WHAT OTHERS ARE
BUYING A FR

"This is not an academic study on fran
on what franchising is, how it works in the UK, typical pitfalls, and a lot of sound advice on how to find a franchise that 'fits'. It is targeted at prospective franchisees but will also be of interest to those considering franchising their businesses. Len writes from personal experience and illustrates many of the points he makes with personal anecdotes. A useful resource for those new to the world of franchising!"

Iain Martin QFP – *Mr Franchise*

"What I really like about this book is that it is written in plain English, well-signposted and well-constructed. It's an excellent reference book and guide book which I wish had been around at the time I became a franchisee. It accurately identifies the pitfalls as well as the many advantages. Franchises have a good record compared with brand new start-up businesses and this book makes it clear that they work, providing you are prepared to follow the system. Anyone who knows anything about franchises will recognise that Len Rainford really knows what he's talking about from a franchisor's and a franchisee's perspectives. It's a piece of common sense writing but, of course, common sense is not always common."

Alistair Macdonald FRG – *AMTV Media*

"The direction of the book, focusing on successful franchising from the perspective of franchisees, is a much needed contribution for the franchise sector. This is an excellent book."

Dr Lola Dada – *Associate Editor of the Journal of Small Business Management & Senior Lecturer at the Department of Entrepreneurship, Strategy and Innovation, Management School, Lancaster University*

"Len Rainford's franchising advice is always honest, straightforward and leavened with a touch of humour. If you are considering buying a franchise, listen to Len."

Linda Whitney – *Daily Mail franchise columnist*

WHAT THEY SAY ABOUT LEN RAINFORD, THE FRANCHISE SPECIALIST

"I have sought Len's advice on franchising on several occasions and he has always pointed me in the right direction. He is an expert in his field with a wealth of experience, and his knowledge in this sector is second to none."

Andy Mault, Managing Director – *Sollertia*

"Len is an exceptional business person and I have had the pleasure of working with him for around 3 years. It's nice to work with someone like Len: friendly, approachable and he does what he says he is going to do."

Joel Bissitt, Franchise Consultant and Business Advisor – *Franchise UK*

"We have had Len Rainford as our franchise consultant for over 2 years now. He is an excellent consultant for our company as he is very knowledgeable and extremely efficient in everything he does. I would definitely recommend Len to anybody who is looking to work with him."

Alan Spaven, Owner – *Spavens*

"I was on a brilliant training course today about franchising businesses, which was run by Len Rainford. Very good, very professional, and highly recommended to business owners looking to expand their operations and increase turnover."

Richard Howard – *AHome4U*

"I have known Len for over 10 years. In that time he has become a close mentor and confidant. His expertise in how to develop a business in my opinion is unrivalled and I have met a lot of so-called business gurus. Anyone involved with Len on a business basis or otherwise can count themselves lucky — a truly brilliant bloke."

Steve Lythe, Managing Director – *Alchemy Advisory Services Ltd*

"The entrepreneurs in residence were absolutely fantastic, particularly our seminar tutor, Len Rainford."

MBA Student – *Lancaster University*

BUYING A FRANCHISE

THE KEYS TO SUCCESS

BY LEN RAINFORD

Buying a Franchise – The Keys to Success

First published 2018

Copyright © 2018 Len Rainford

Published by JOADOM Publishing

Cover design and typesetting by Tanya Back

Edited by Siân-Elin Flint-Freel

Printed and bound by Ingram Spark

ISBN: 978-1-9164835-0-7

"I dedicate this book to all the people that I have met in my life who have helped me, encouraged me, and inspired me to be successful, both in my personal life and in business, people who have been there for me both in the good times and the bad, my family and close friends. There are far too many to name, but these people use their knowledge and influence to help others and make the world a better place.

I hope that the information and ideas in this book help you to achieve the success that you are seeking and enable you to lead a happy and fulfilled life."

CONTENTS

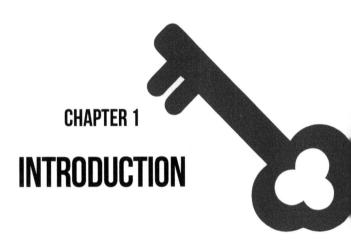

CHAPTER 1

INTRODUCTION

I decided to write this book after a conversation with a business owner who was thinking about franchising her business. She told me that she had read two books about franchising and quite frankly they had confused her and had put her off.

Similarly, I have lost count of the number of conversations that I have had with people who haven't a clue what franchising is about. I have done talks at schools and academies to students studying business, but when I ask them what they know about franchising I am invariably met with a blank look or "Is it McDonald's?" I asked one tutor why this was and the answer was simple — "We don't teach franchising." In the UK, there are only a handful of universities that have a franchise module, so is it any wonder that there is a lack of knowledge about the subject?

Despite the fact that franchising accounts for over £15.1 billion of the UK's economy [1], and most people come into direct contact with

1   NatWest/BFA survey

several franchises every day, there is still a huge lack of understanding about what franchising is and how it works.

CASE STUDY
FRANCHISES IN MANY SECTORS

Consider this: Joanne and Paul get up early every morning. They have an 11-year-old daughter, Abbey, and a 2-year-old son, Andrew. Paul needs to get up early because he is a delivery driver for *Speedy Freight* and often skips breakfast until after he has loaded his van at the depot. This morning he pops into *McDonald's* for a quick breakfast before setting off on his deliveries. Paul's van has just had two new tyres which were fitted outside his house by *etyres* because he didn't have the time to take it to a garage. One of his late morning deliveries is to *HomeXperts*, the estate agents, which is close to *Subway*, so he pops in there for his lunch. One of his afternoon deliveries is to *Signs Express*: big heavy boxes that sap his energy. Back at the depot he gives Jo a quick call; he knows how busy she is, so he tells her he will pick up a pizza from *Papa John's* on his way home. Jo works evenings in a local pub owned by *Marstons*. This morning, she went to *Kids Collective* nursery to see about booking Andrew in when he turns three. On the way home she met up with her sister Alison for a coffee in *Starbucks*, but couldn't stay long as the guy from *TruGreen* was coming to mow the lawns and *ChipsAway* were coming to repair some scratches on the car. Abbey, meanwhile, went straight from school to her local *Mathsnasium* where she is working hard to improve her maths. Tonight is Jo's night off, so Paul takes the opportunity to meet up with his football mates at *Anytime Fitness* for a quick workout.

I am sure that most of you can relate to that story. What you may not realise is that every company mentioned operates a franchise. In the UK, there are now over 900 franchise brands covering 80 different sectors[2] — there is something for everyone.

Franchising can be a complex business and understanding it clearly is essential for success, but it doesn't have to be complicated. This book will explain how franchising works and will tackle some of the myths that have built up over the years, as well as guide you through the process of starting and running your own successful franchise. Finally, although it seems odd to include the thought of leaving or selling your franchise before you even start, this book will also help you to consider your exit strategy. Throughout this book I will speak in plain English, explain things clearly and not use any jargon. There is enough to get your head around without having to learn a whole new language as well!

2   NatWest/BFA survey

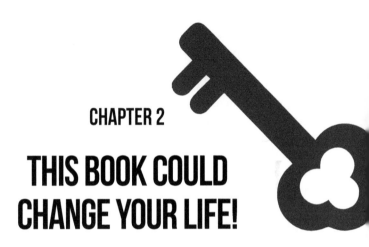

CHAPTER 2

THIS BOOK COULD CHANGE YOUR LIFE!

OK, maybe that is a bit of a bold statement, but it will certainly help you from making some unnecessary and costly mistakes. It will also help you to work through problems to do with your business that are keeping you awake at night.

This book will benefit both potential franchisees who are starting from scratch and existing franchisees. Even if you are one of the latter and may have experience in running your own franchise, there is always room for improvement. It will help you to assess your current situation, improve your performance, make your franchise even more productive, maybe expand and become even more successful.

Potential franchisees

Maybe you have been thinking about running your own business but don't want to start from scratch with a new venture. Some will have always wanted to run their own business, but for whatever reason they have never taken the plunge. There are several reasons for this, including lack of financial resources, marriage, children, being in a good job, not being able to find a good idea or the right franchise, tending to be risk averse or having a lack of confidence. All of these things can prevent someone taking the plunge, packing in their job and going self-employed, starting a business or buying a franchise.

Existing franchisees

Existing franchisees will also benefit from reading this book. They may be in a franchise that they are not happy with and looking elsewhere. Maybe they didn't do enough research and ask the right questions. They may be happy with their franchise but find things in this book that prompts them to look at other franchises, ask questions of their current franchisor and compare them. This could also result in an improvement in their current franchise. They may be coming to the end of their agreement and simply want a change. This book will help them to assess other franchises by asking all the right questions. Finally, they may want to sell their franchise but don't have an exit strategy.

WHO BECOMES A FRANCHISEE?

As already mentioned, there are many reasons that people put off running their own business, be it starting a family, fear or lacking in confidence, along with the others listed previously. This is reflected in the average age of franchisees, which is between 45 and 55[3], although this is reducing slightly each year as more and more younger people are wanting to run their own business. There is also an increase in the number of women in franchising. Often when people reach that age several things change in their life. Their children become less dependent, they may get divorced, they may be fed up with their job or corporate life, they may get made redundant (or choose to take voluntary redundancy), they may take early semi-retirement, or they just might be having a mid-life crisis! From a financial point of view, their mortgage may be less, their cost of living may be reduced, they might have a nice redundancy package, or they may have been left a tidy lump sum. They are now in a position where they can look at the various options open to them, assess them and make calculated decisions.

---

3   NatWest/BFA survey

Most people are well aware of the risk involved in starting their own business. However, franchising significantly reduces that risk. It gives the franchisee the opportunity to own and run a business with a proven business format and an established brand. It provides all the essential elements for running a successful business, except for one key ingredient, the person who will run the business – You.

Often, though, people looking at buying a franchise do so through 'rose-tinted spectacles'. They are overwhelmed by it all, they get carried away with excitement, they believe all the hype and everything that they are told, and don't do enough research. I met one guy at a business network meeting who said, "I wish I had met you two years earlier." He had bought a franchise that he wasn't enjoying. It was in fact a good established franchise and had won several awards; the problem was, it didn't suit him and he wasn't enjoying it. He was responsible for attracting customers and he wasn't comfortable with this sales role. He is happy now in a franchise where the majority of customers come to him because it is a well-known coffee shop franchise. Quite simply he hadn't asked the right questions, not just about the franchise but about himself: What did he really want? Why did he want it? What would make him happy? He hadn't looked into it fully from every angle and he hadn't done sufficient research.

New franchisees tend to fall into three categories, sometimes referred to as 'the good, the bad and the ugly'. A little bit unfair in some cases, but nevertheless often true.

The first category is generally someone who has always wanted to run their own business, but for the reasons previously stated has never done it. Very often, but not always, these are people that have worked in sales or management, people that are sociable and good communicators or people that have a specific transferable skill. People who have been in the armed forces or the police force are generally good at being franchisees because they are disciplined and used to following systems and procedures. They are motivated, not just by money but by a strong sense of achievement and a desire for success.

The second category is typified by someone who has been made redundant after working for the same organisation for many years and can't get a job. Once this type of person reaches the level of income that he was earning in his job, he switches off, he is in his comfort zone. They are not necessarily a 'bad' franchisee but they could do a lot better. Again, this is not always the case. However, it can be very frustrating for a franchisor when a franchisee is not making the most of a lucrative territory. A franchisee who is under performing could be missing out on a lot of potential business in an area, whereas a more proactive franchisee will make the most of the opportunity to increase the business. Just one of the reasons why areas and territories can be a contentious issue.

The third category applies to people who just shouldn't buy a franchise in the first place: people who think it will be an easy ride and are living in cloud cuckoo land, people who are not prepared to follow the system and put the effort in. I know that it seems unbelievable as they have probably parted with a substantial sum of money, but, believe me, they do exist, although usually not for long. As a franchisee you have a responsibility to be honest with yourself and to look at the skills and knowledge needed for the franchise and then decide if you have what it takes for that franchise. More about that in Chapter 6.

Sometimes the franchisor is to blame for not having a specific franchisee profile, or is quite happy to take a franchise fee off anyone, regardless of their lack of knowledge, experience or past record. This tends to apply more to new franchises who haven't done enough groundwork rather than the established franchises. Most franchisors are ethical and recognise the dangers of taking someone on just because they have the money. Existing franchisees become the testimonials for future recruitment and if you have a few bad ones it can have a serious negative effect on the growth of the network. Although franchising is very successful, each year around 100 new franchises come to market, while around the same number fail or stop franchising for one reason or another. These include taking on people who are not suitable to run the franchise and failing because they have not taken professional advice. They have gone ahead without having all the necessary documents, systems and processes in place.

If you are seriously looking at buying a franchise, this book will be a great benefit to you. It will guide you through the steps you need to take, the questions you need to ask and the research you need to do so that you will make the right decision for you.

If I can help one potential franchisee to find the right franchise, or stop one potential franchisee from joining a poorly prepared franchise, then all the time and effort in writing this book will be time well spent.

SIX QUESTIONS

From a very young age I have used a well-known poem by Rudyard Kipling to guide me through life and solve many problems. It is simple but so effective and I will refer to it again throughout this book. The first four lines are the key:

> "I keep six honest serving men,
> They taught me all I knew.
> Their names are What and Why and When,
> And How and Where and Who."

If you have a problem or need a solution for something, ask yourself those six questions; they will make you think, come up with answers and, believe me, they will be a great help.

So, my first six questions to you are:

What made you pick up this book?

Why are you reading it?

When will you finish it?

How will you set aside time to record and work on the actions that you want to take?

Where do you want to be in 1/5/10 years' time?

Who are the best people to help you achieve your goals?

You may not know all the answers yet, but keep these questions in mind as you continue to read. Many people read books once and then put them on the shelf to gather dust and never touch them again. Most of us have done it. I have shelves full of books I haven't touched for years. I also have books that I have read over and over again, books that helped me to learn, which have given me lots of value and benefit, books that have helped me along the way in my journey. I also have books that I refer to from time to time when I need certain information.

However, I learned early on that one of the best ways to get value from a book was to complete any exercises at the end of each chapter, and then read it again, review the exercises and implement any actions. Sometimes you need to return to a book once you have completed your actions to see how much you have learned and to maybe start the process again so that you are always learning and improving.

Your learning style is up to you, but I would recommend that you take the time to read the questions I pose at the end of each chapter. They will help you to become successful in the franchise of your choice.

Congratulations, you have taken the first step. I hope that you enjoy this book, and more importantly, I hope that it helps you in your franchising journey.

 # EXERCISE:

Ask yourself the following questions:

What made you pick up this book?

Why are you reading it?

When will you finish it?

How will you set aside time to record and work on the actions you want to take?

Where do you want to be in 1/5/10 years' time?

Who are the best people to help you achieve your goals?

 # ACTIVITY:

In one sentence, record what you want to achieve from reading this book and set yourself a timescale e.g.

I will decide which franchise I want to join by January 2019.

I will improve the profit in my franchise in the next 12 months.

I will sell my existing franchise by 31st December 2019.

"TO ACCOMPLISH GREAT THINGS, WE MUST NOT ONLY ACT, BUT ALSO DREAM; NOT ONLY PLAN, BUT ALSO BELIEVE."

Anatole France

CHAPTER 3

THE HISTORY OF FRANCHISING

Before we go into the detail of franchising, let's have a look at the interesting history and background.

LET'S BEGIN AT THE BEGINNING...

The first signs of franchising can be traced back to feudal England, when lords allowed peasants certain rights on part of their land in return for a fee (to perform tasks such as operating wells for water provision or running a market, for example). Components of a franchise system could also be found in the provision of resources for an army by local lords and chiefs in return for tax-collecting privileges.

Many years later, franchising became more entrenched in the UK with the advent of the tied pub system. Following the introduction of legislation making it very expensive to keep and maintain a public house in the 18th century, licensees began to struggle to operate successfully. Recognising that it was in their interests to have a secure and stable market for their products, brewers began to offer publicans the opportunity of financial support in return for exclusivity over what was sold in the pub.

Thus, a familiar system that remains widely used in the licensed trade today was born.

THE SINGER EFFECT

The origins of franchising as it's come to be known and defined today can be clearly pinpointed to one man: Isaac Singer. After the US Civil War in the 1860s Singer had achieved the ability to mass-produce his famous sewing machines, but had no economically viable way of repairing and maintaining them across a country as vast as the USA.

He began to license out servicing and repairs to local merchants around the country, who were later permitted to become regional salesmen for the machines too. Singer's use of a contract for this arrangement introduced the earliest form of franchise agreements, and the first modern franchise system was born.

Over the following century, forms of franchising became more widely used in the US as a way to systemise products and standards from one coast to another. First was the car dealership model pioneered by General Motors in the early 1900s, granting exclusive rights and territories to franchise business owners; then oil companies and grocery stores began to take advantage of a business model that offered them a route of fast growth towards national distribution with reduced risk.

BUSINESS FORMAT FRANCHISING IS BORN

After the Second World War, franchising grew rapidly, propelled by companies looking to expand quickly. Soft drinks giants like Coca-Cola and Pepsi couldn't operate economically US-wide with such high water content in their products and expensive transportation relative to its cost, so they developed a franchise system whereby franchisees would carbonate and add water to the centrally manufactured and distributed highly secretive syrup recipes, bottling and selling it locally.

This was the start of 'business format franchising' as we now know it today, franchisors offering a ready-made package to franchisees. In many instances, it was established as a distinct business model and proven system in the 1950s. The huge growth in this modern system of franchising is attributed to milkshake machine salesman Ray Kroc who, while visiting San Bernardino in California, frequented a popular and busy drive-thru restaurant that had bought his machines – which was owned and run by the McDonald brothers. He opened the first restaurant in their name in Des Plaines, Illinois (and purchased the brand outright in 1961).

UK BOOM AND SLOWDOWN

In the 1950s and 1960s the popularity of franchising really took off in the USA, in tandem with huge growths in population, economic output and social change, and franchises began to appear internationally, including in the UK for the first time. Catering companies led the way.

Amongst the earliest practitioners in the UK was food giant J Lyons & Co., who franchised the hamburger chain Wimpy in 1955, as well as ice-cream brands Lyons Maid and Mr Softee in the same decade. ServiceMaster, still a huge international franchise business today, began franchising in the UK in 1959. By the mid-1960s some of the largest fast-food brands had become well-established international franchises, led by McDonald's and Kentucky Fried Chicken.

This boom period in franchising was not to last long. By the 1970s franchising in the UK slowed, partly in response to the faltering economy, but more as a result of the damage done to its reputation by non-franchise systems such as pyramid schemes describing themselves as franchises; they were based around the handing over of money for a promised lucrative return on investment which, of course, rarely came. Despite still offering some real opportunities, franchising was tarred unfairly with the same brush and its popularity waned.

FRANCHISORS FIGHT BACK!

Eight of the largest franchise brands in the UK at the time decided they needed to do something to differentiate their own ethical business practices from those companies with bad ethics or little integrity and, as a result, in 1977 the British Franchise Association (BFA) was formed.

The founding member companies of the BFA were ServiceMaster, Dyno-Rod, Holiday Inns UK, Kentucky Fried Chicken, Wimpy International, Ziebart GB, Prontaprint and Budget Rent a Car.

With no previous set standards in the UK, the industry thus created its own regulatory body and accredited a company's suitability for membership on strict criteria related to operational practices, business procedures, franchise agreement terms and the support offered to franchisees.

The size and stature of these founding members and the BFA's early work on business ethics restored credibility to the business model and, with the economic boom of the 1980s and 1990s, many new brands came into UK franchising and remain there today, including Signarama and Papa John's.

By the mid-eighties the BFA had grown and developed, but already recognised the need to encapsulate the professional advisors from the industry into the Association. This would not only allow the industry to bring the professional advisors into the same fold with regards to best practice, but it would also allow potential clients to identify those advisors working to BFA standards. Therefore, in 1985 the Affiliate membership was created for professional advisors in franchising, which included banks, solicitors, consultants, media and various specialist suppliers.

FRANCHISING TODAY

Franchising has since flourished into an industry which now has nearly 1,000 brands in a multitude of different sectors. Long gone are the days when it revolved around cars and catering, and nowadays its eclectic mix of businesses includes everything from hairdressing to photography, pet care to children's sport coaching. There's something to suit your passion, whatever it may be.

Franchising has never been in better health than it is now. The authoritative annual research into the state of the industry, the BFA/

NatWest Franchise Survey,[4] has shown both short- and long-term growth trends to be very strong in the sector, including, prior to and since the economic downturn in 2008.

After a slight downturn in that year, each subsequent year has shown growth in terms of numbers of brands franchising, numbers of franchisees, numbers employed in franchise businesses and the overall turnover of the franchise sector.

These figures combine with impressive trends going back to before the turn of the century, uninterrupted by the recession, which consistently show around 90% of franchisees reporting profitability and less than 4% of franchise businesses failing for commercial reasons each year.

These statistics compare favourably to figures estimating that between half and two-thirds of all independent start-ups close within their first 3 years. It's clear that the advantages inherent within a franchise business, including economies of scale and the support of a large brand combined with local marketing and business owners with a knowledge of their area, make them particularly robust and statistically much more likely to succeed.

BFA/NAT WEST SURVEY 2016

In 2015 franchising set a number of new records as its performance continued a remarkable rise over the decade. New benchmarks in turnover, profitability, numbers of franchisee-owned businesses and jobs created by the sector highlight the important and growing contribution of franchising to the UK's economy.

The contribution of franchising to the UK economy is now reckoned to be around **£15.1 billion**, an increase of 46% over the past 10 years and up 10% since the previous BFA/ NatWest survey in 2013.

---

4 The BFA/NatWest Franchise survey is available from the British Franchise Association

The total number of people employed in franchising in the UK is **621,000**, of which 321,000 are in full-time employment. This equates to an increase of 70% over the past 10 years.

The number of franchisee-owned businesses increased by 14% in two years, to **44,200.** On average, those businesses are also becoming larger as the sector matures.

Average turnover continues to rise and over half claim an annual turnover of more than **£250,000**.

Employment per unit continues its upwards trajectory, with **one-third employing 10 or more staff**.

A record **97%** of franchisee-owned units reported profitability, with **56%** saying they are 'quite' or 'very' profitable.

Ownership changes in franchisee businesses are correspondingly low (**4.6%**), with failure rates at around **3%**, much lower than for other SMEs where the failure rate is around **45%** in the first year.

Franchisees' satisfaction with their franchisor has never been higher, with **91%** saying they are 'mainly' or 'definitely' satisfied.

80% of franchise brands in this country are UK-owned and developed. Some **29%** of franchisees now run multiple units.

The number of franchise brands operating in the UK is now 901 and covers around 80 different sectors.

CURRENT TRENDS

One in five franchisees who launched their business in the last two years was under 30 years old when they did so. There has also been an increase in the number of female franchisees.

From my experience over the past few years I am sure that this trend of younger franchise owners will continue, and I can see several reasons for it. There are no longer 'jobs for life', people want more flexibility, more young people want to work for themselves and more are becoming aware of franchising as a suitable business model with less risk than starting from scratch. For the same reasons, the number of females is also increasing as they thrive in an entrepreneurial environment. Both men and women have career breaks to start a family and no longer want to work for someone else. Many also see franchising as a way to control their working hours and to have a better work/life balance.

Franchising offers a multitude of opportunities that can be operated full-time or part-time to fit in with a person's lifestyle. There is something for everyone — just make sure you find one that you enjoy and makes you happy.

THE FUTURE

Modern franchising now covers a vast array of business sectors, both Business to Business (B2B) and Business to Consumer (B2C), blue collar and white collar, from home-based operations to some of the world's most recognised brands. The chances are that most people use the services of a franchise business each week either personally or professionally, even if they don't realise it at the time, as illustrated in the example in the introduction.

One of the biggest recent changes in franchising occurred in 2012, with the advent of Franchisee Membership to the BFA. Franchisees were given the opportunity of direct representation on the board of the BFA, thereby being able to contribute to the future evolution and governance of their industry. It marked the first membership scheme of its kind for any franchising association in the world, and ensures that all stakeholders of ethical franchising can continue to move the UK industry forwards as it continues to grow in size, stature and in its importance to the economy.

From its feudal roots to becoming one of the fastest-growing sectors of the UK economy, franchising has come a long way. With many more people now looking to take charge of their careers and family life by running their own business, it looks set to go a whole lot further in the years to come too.

EXERCISE:

Ask yourself the following question:

Franchising has changed and developed over the years. Are you prepared to change?

ACTIVITY:

Write down the 5 things you want to change in your life, e.g. more flexibility in your working day, less travel for work, more control in your working life, your work/life balance (even if it means a possible reduction in income and working from home), becoming the sales director, marketing manager, administrator, accountant etc of your own business

1.

2.

3.

4.

5.

"IF YOU ALWAYS DO WHAT YOU'VE ALWAYS DONE, YOU WILL ALWAYS GET WHAT YOU'VE ALWAYS GOT."

Henry Ford

CHAPTER 4

WHAT IS FRANCHISING?

Clearly understanding franchising and what being a franchisee or a franchisor means is essential to the success of your business.

DEFINITIONS

The **British Franchise Association** (BFA) definition of franchising states:

"Franchising is a system of marketing goods and/or services and/or technology, which is based upon a close and ongoing collaboration between legally and financially separate and independent undertakings, the franchisor and its individual franchisees. The franchisor grants its individual franchisees the right, and imposes the obligation, to conduct a business in accordance with the franchisor's concept. The right entitles and compels the individual franchisee, in exchange for a direct or indirect financial consideration, to use the franchisor's trade name, and/or trade mark and/or service mark, know-how, business and technical methods, procedural system, and other industrial and/or intellectual property rights. This is supported by the continuing provision of commercial and technical assistance, within the framework and for the term of a written franchise agreement, concluded between parties for this purpose."

The **Business Dictionary** definition states:

"An arrangement where one party (the franchisor) grants another party (the franchisee) the right to use its trademark or trade-name as well as certain business systems and processes, to produce and market goods or services according to certain specifications. The franchisee usually pays a one-time franchise fee plus a percentage of sales revenue as royalty, and gains (1) immediate name recognition, (2) tried and tested products, (3) standard building design and décor, (4) detailed techniques in running and promoting the business, (5) training of employees, and (6) ongoing help in promoting and upgrading of the products."

The **Oxford English Dictionary** definition of franchising states:

"The business or activity of giving or selling franchises to people", a franchise being defined as "Formal permission given by a company to somebody who wants to sell its goods or services in a particular area."

Putting it simply, franchising is a relationship where one party — the franchisor — allows another party — the franchisee — to operate copies or clones of a proven business model in return for initial and ongoing fees. The franchisee will generally be given an exclusive area or territory for a defined period of time.

In effect, the franchisor allows the franchisee to operate a branch of its business using the proven methods, processes, systems and brand. This gives the franchisee a head-start in setting up their business because the sales and administration processes are already in place and, in many cases, the brand will already be well known. The franchisee will be expected to operate the business in accordance with those proven systems and not do anything to adversely affect the brand.

In return, the franchisee will be required to pay both the initial and ongoing fees. The ongoing fees are usually determined as a percentage of the franchisee's turnover and may vary from a small percentage of 4 - 5% up to (and sometimes in excess of) 20%, dependent upon the level of support provided by the franchisor. These higher levels often apply where the franchisor provides a number of additional services, for example, invoicing and credit control and, in some cases, finding new customers and sales opportunities for the franchisee.

HOW IT WORKS

One of the key attributes of franchising is that the franchisee will continue to receive advice, training, and support from the franchisor throughout the term of the franchise, thus improving their chances of operating a successful business. Whilst no franchisor can ever guarantee that their franchisees will be successful, it is certainly true to say that they are likely to be more successful than if they had started a new business on their own.

There is a wide variety of business models within the franchise sector. For example, in some franchises it is the parent company, the franchisor, that invoices the customer and collects the money, while in others it is the franchisee. Some companies charge a management service fee, some a marketing fee, some both and it is often a % of turnover, as mentioned previously. Deciding which model suits you best takes time and effort and getting it right from the beginning is crucial in avoiding costly mistakes. I will talk more about which franchise is best for you in Chapter 7.

Many national and international brands have been created through franchising, Anytime Fitness, Chips Away, ServiceMaster and Subway to name but a few. It can take a long time to build a national brand, but it can be done a lot quicker through franchising by replicating your business in other towns and cities. Many franchisors encourage their franchisees to take on multiple units, enabling growth for both parties.

All reputable franchisors will have a franchise agreement which sets out all the legal obligations of both parties. There will be more about this in Chapter 8 — The franchisor/franchisee relationship.

WHAT FRANCHISING ISN'T

In the early days, franchising was often categorised with pyramid selling, which wrongly damaged its reputation, and later with network marketing. It is neither of these.

Network or Multilevel marketing involves recruiting individuals to work for a company. In this type of marketing you generate income from the products you sell and from the sales of those you recruit. Pyramid selling is similar, but often there are no products involved and you only generate income from the people you recruit.

Franchising involves purchasing a complete business format from an already established company. When you purchase a franchise, you have access to the company's business model, advertising and products or services. In addition, you often receive support and training from the company.

Make no mistake, franchising is not an easy option. There is no golden chalice. Even with an established, well-known brand it requires hard work, dedication, discipline and a determination to succeed. However, with plenty of effort, commitment, enthusiasm and drive franchising can be one of the best ways of running your own business.

WHAT IS A FRANCHISOR?

A franchisor is the company owning and controlling the rights to grant franchises to potential franchisees.

Almost any business that can operate a branch network can be franchised. However, as with any business venture, there is risk involved and it must be done right.

Whatever the business does before it is franchised — cleaning, coffee shop, courier service, fast food, hair and beauty — is somewhat irrelevant when it becomes a franchisor. Most of the elements needed to run any successful business are the same: accounts, admin, finance, operations, sales and marketing, staff, and customer service. But the job of the franchisor is to recruit, train, monitor, support and motivate people. It becomes a different business.

Franchising is a term that some business owners regard with anticipation and excitement and others with fear and trepidation. The truth is that franchising is one of the most significant, stable, and sustainable growth strategies that a business can implement. However, the excitement and possible benefits of franchising a business can result in some business owners taking the leap before putting everything into place to ensure it is successful and advantageous to both the franchisor and the franchisee. This is why it is so important to do your homework before choosing a franchise to ensure that everything is in place and is right for you and will give you every chance of succeeding in your new venture.

ROLE OF THE FRANCHISOR

A franchisor has five major responsibilities for the success of the franchise system:

- To recruit the right calibre of franchisee. All franchisors should have a profile of an ideal franchisee. Is it someone practical? Is it white collar? Is it customer facing? Having said that, it doesn't pay to be overly dismissive. I have met several people over the years who have decided on a complete career change, doing something that they had never done before, and have become successful. However, it is a mistake to take on someone just because they are willing to pay the franchise fee.

- To provide new franchisees with an initial training course covering every aspect of the business to ensure that they are competent from day one.

- To provide on-going training and support. This can come in many forms: field visits, phone calls, webinars, seminars and workshops.

- To monitor franchisees' performance and act accordingly. This is essential, particularly in the early days. It helps to spot any weaknesses and any areas that can be improved, and also to reward franchisees for their performance.

- To motivate franchisees to be successful and achieve their goals. Not everyone's goals will be the same. For some it will be about how much money they can make, for others it will be more about lifestyle.

WHAT IS A FRANCHISEE?

A franchisee is a person or company that is granted the right to conduct business under the franchisor's trademark, trade name, and business model, in a specified location, area or territory by the franchisor.

In return for the right to operate the franchise, the franchisee will pay an initial franchise fee and an on-going royalty or commission.

The franchisee then operates the business in the specified location, area, or territory. He or she is responsible for certain decisions, but many other decisions, such as the brand, name, products or services, are already determined by the franchisor and must be kept the same by the franchisee. The franchisee will pay the franchisor under the terms of the agreement, usually either a flat fee or a percentage of the revenues or profits, from the sales transacted through the franchise. They may also be required to pay a Management Service fee or a Marketing fee, or both.

ROLE OF THE FRANCHISEE

A franchisee has five major responsibilities for the success of the franchise system:

- To implement the standard working practices of the franchisor and improve on them.

- To protect the franchised brand by operating the franchise in strict compliance with the system operating standards.

- To build a strong and loyal customer base by offering only approved products and services and by providing superior customer service.

- To ensure that all employees are properly trained as per the operations and training manuals, and that the franchise is properly staffed at all times.

- To advertise and promote the franchise and its approved products and services as stated in the guidelines provided by the franchisor.

ATTRIBUTES OF A SUCCESSFUL FRANCHISEE

History has shown that successful franchisees tend to possess certain key traits. As you become more committed to the idea of pursuing a franchise opportunity, it is important that you take some time to analyse yourself from a business and personal perspective. You need to identify which traits you possess, as well as those you demonstrate. However, a well-structured franchise system will provide a level of support that contributes to the success of the franchise.

Although the skills and attributes required to become a successful franchisee are as varied as the types of franchises available, there are some which are common across the board.

Be willing and able to learn new skills. As a franchisee, you will take on a multitude of roles, including training, management, customer service, sales and finance. The franchisor sets the brand standards, but they are not totally responsible for how the franchisee's day-to-day business is run. That is the responsibility of the franchisee. It is a steep learning curve, but if you can master these new skills, you can become a successful franchisee.

Be able and willing to follow system standards. As a franchisee, you are agreeing to follow someone else's operating system, often including specific requirements for what marketing materials to use, which suppliers you must work with, and what specific products or services you must offer. This, along with the rights and restrictions on how you can use the franchisor's intellectual property, is what you are investing in.

In exchange for this ready-made operating system, a franchisee generally has to report their sales and expenses, follow instructions on how to present the products and services, and comply with the franchisor's marketing requirements. If the franchisee fails to meet those brand standards, they risk being in breach of their franchise agreement.

Be ready to move from employment into running a business. Employees who wants to become a franchisee need to understand the implications. You may have a broad understanding of business, know how to work within a system, know how to motivate staff, and certainly are no stranger to long hours, but a franchisee is essentially a small business owner, which means leaving behind the internal support services you have grown accustomed to, as well as the many benefits that come with employment at a larger company, such as retirement plans and paid sick days, expense accounts, and health insurance plans. One of the key areas of any business is sales and marketing, and it is often one of the areas that a new franchisee finds difficult. In their previous work, they may have had a marketing department and sales people generating the business, now they have to do it themselves. It is also one of the reasons why someone who has worked in sales and marketing often make good franchisees.

As a franchisee, your success is measured by the performance of your franchise, requiring more self-reliance than many corporate managers have had to demonstrate previously as an employee. However, a well-structured franchise system will provide a level of support that contributes to the success of the franchise.

A strong and effective business relationship between franchisee and franchisor is critical to the success of both businesses and the franchise system overall. Personally, I think that this relationship is so important that I have dedicated a whole chapter to the subject later in the book (Chapter 8).

EXERCISE:

Ask yourself the following question:

Am I really ready to move from my current situation into running a business? (i.e. moving from employment/being a homemaker/ changing from part-time or seasonal employment etc.)

ACTIVITY:

Fill in the table below which lists the main attributes needed for a franchisee. Be absolutely honest with yourself, because you will only be fooling yourself if you don't think it through.

Attribute	Questions to ask yourself	Do I have this attribute? Y/N	What do I need to do to make sure I have this attribute?
Willing and able to learn new skills	Do I have the time? Do I have the space to learn? Do I like learning new things? Which of these skills do I already possess? training, management, customer service, sales and finance		

Attribute	Questions to ask yourself	Do I have this attribute? Y/N	What do I need to do to make sure I have this attribute?
Willing and able to follow system standards	Am I good at following instructions? Do I find it difficult to do what I am told?		
Ready to move into running your own business	Can I use my own initiative? Can I cope without a regular income for a few months? How will I cope with sick days? What would I do about my pension/retirement plan/health insurance?		

"YOU MAY NEVER KNOW WHAT RESULTS COME OF YOUR ACTION, BUT IF YOU DO NOTHING THERE WILL BE NO RESULT."

Mahatma Gandhi

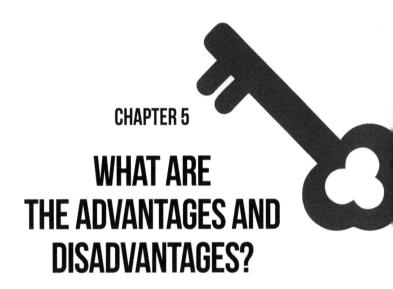

CHAPTER 5

WHAT ARE THE ADVANTAGES AND DISADVANTAGES?

WHY CONSIDER BUYING A FRANCHISE V STARTING YOUR OWN BUSINESS?

Basically, it comes down to risk and belief. Buying into an existing and proven business model is an attractive proposition. You can see how it works and what it can deliver in terms of revenue and profits. With the exception of new franchises, you can talk to existing franchisees to get reassurance that it is indeed a good business opportunity.

If your definition of success is becoming filthy rich, buying a franchise business could get you there...but it may not. Although franchise ownership can provide a proven business model with instant brand awareness, it doesn't always result in wealth. For that kind of success, you need to take on a franchise that's in demand with consumers, you will need to employ strong people skills and, of course, put in the hours learning everything about the company — even so, there is no guarantee of success in any business. What I am saying is that if you put in the effort and chose your franchise wisely, you stand a better chance of getting there — much more so than buying a lottery ticket!

It may be tough to turn a franchise business into big money, but it's not impossible. Many franchisees now have multiple outlets. The franchising industry regularly likes to remind us that being a franchisee is a safe and potentially very profitable way of getting into business. This is true and the statistics speak for themselves but, while this may be true, there are also downsides.

ADVANTAGES OF FRANCHISING

Proven system

Franchising offers you a much safer route into business, as your 'Business Blueprint' has been tried and tested, thus avoiding many of the pitfalls of a new start up. Also, franchising combines the expertise of an established company with the commitment and entrepreneurial flare of the individual.

Own operation

You own your own operation but have the benefit of a recognised brand name and the associated products or services.

The Franchise package

At the outset, you will receive everything that you need to run your business: accounting systems, administration procedures, marketing material and guidance, and an operations manual. This will save you both time and money. Where appropriate, you may also benefit from the bulk buying capacity of the franchisor.

Ongoing help and support

Most franchisors provide initial and on-going training programmes and support. As well, they will often help you to find and retain customers and provide accounting and stock control systems. The level of assistance varies depending on the franchisor but generally franchisees are not left to struggle alone. After all, it is in the interests of the franchisor to help franchisees to become successful.

Big names can lead to big success

Franchising under a well-known brand such as McDonald's or Subway has obvious benefits for franchisees. Not only are you following a tried and tested format, you can also benefit from the financial aspects of the larger corporations when it comes to funding a franchise. Most of the major banks will lend up to 70% of the total investment in a well-established brand. This increases the security for your enterprise.

You can also save time and energy by not worrying about generating publicity to raise awareness as customers will know what to expect from a big chain.

Having an established market, proven systems and a respected business name means that the battle is already half won for you before you even start your first day of trading.

However, a word of caution, not all franchises are 'Big Names', some are in the early stages of development and require lots of due diligence. You should give this careful consideration before buying such a franchise. If you are willing to put the effort and shoe leather into promoting the business and have a personality which is suited to attracting people and customers, then this is not a problem. If the thought of doing heavy marketing scares you, maybe a new or relatively new franchise is not for you.

Defined territory

The BFA lists this as one of the main reasons that franchising is an attractive option. Franchisors carefully choose the location of their outlets to gain the largest possible amount of custom and to avoid franchisees treading on each other's toes.

Also, unlike starting a business from scratch, many franchisors can afford prime trading premises, such as on the high street and popular shopping centres.

Greater access to finance:

As a franchisee, you are looked upon more favourably when it comes to bank loans and overdrafts than if you were a struggling entrepreneur trying to kick-start your own firm from scratch. The increased security and reliability of an established company behind you means that banks will often offer you substantial loans to fund your start-up.

Less risk

Because franchised businesses have been tried and tested and proved to work, the risk of your business failing is greatly reduced. You will have an established business model with ongoing support.

DISADVANTAGES OF FRANCHISING

Initial and on-going fees

You will be investing in the franchisor's business as well as your own. Franchisors will charge new franchisees an initial lump sum franchise fee for the right to use their brand name. The amount varies greatly depending on the franchisor.

Many will insist that you purchase any stock, equipment or materials that you need upfront, and some will require you to have a certain amount of working capital before you are even considered to be a suitable candidate.

Franchisors will also take a regular slice of your revenue as royalty fees or commission. This is generally a percentage of turnover or a set monthly amount. If you have a tight profit margin this can cause problems. In most cases, you will also have to pay a marketing fee to cover head office advertising and marketing. You may also have to do additional localised marketing at your own cost.

Once your fixed-term contract is up with your franchisor you will generally have to pay a renewal fee to extend the time that you can trade under the company's name. This again will vary.

Although these costs may compare favourably to those you would incur if you were starting up on your own, it is worth remembering that you will often have to deal with all the normal overheads that a business generates, such as rent and rates, wages and insurances. It can all add up to a fairly large amount and you must be sure that you have the necessary capital behind you before you embark on your franchise.

You do things their way, not yours

As mentioned before, each franchisee will benefit from training and guidelines on how the business should be run. Although this is helpful in the early days of running your business, after your franchise is established you may feel your entrepreneurial creativity is somewhat restricted.

You may get slightly frustrated if your plans for your outlet are hampered by company policy on what you can and can't do. For example, you may have a coffee shop franchise and want to stock a cake that is made locally but you are not allowed to by the franchisor. Franchisors generally like their outlets to look and feel the same way, so you will have to work within someone else's idea of what is best for your company.

You may have come up with an idea that you feel will improve a practice or process, such as the stock control, but by and large you have to stick to the business format unless the franchisor is prepared to listen and consider changes.

As well as restricting your independence, the penalties for falling out of line with your franchisor's wishes can be harsh. Many franchise contracts stipulate that any major alterations to the running of your franchise can lead to the termination of your agreement.

Other people's decisions could sink your franchise

The lack of actual overall control you have over your franchise means that even if you run a profitable outlet, you could still lose everything if your franchisor makes bad business decisions and the franchise fails as a whole.

Another potential source of trouble is the actions of other franchisees. One bad franchisee could ruin the good name of the company, dragging down your profits as well as your reputation.

Restrictions

As the success of your business grows, you may want to expand, but are unable to do so because neighbouring areas are already occupied by other franchisees.

Hard work

You cannot escape hard work: If you take on a franchise under the impression that the franchisor will do all of the hard work for you while you sit back and watch the money roll in you will be in for a nasty shock. Working weeks of 60 hours or more are not unheard of among franchisees attempting to get their business off the ground.

Implementing the standard working practices of your franchisor and then building a successful franchise is a massive task and one that takes dedication and a lot of support from family and friends.

EXERCISE:

Ask yourself the following questions:

Do the advantages outweigh the disadvantages in my case?

Is it worth taking the risk?

ACTIVITY:

Go through the advantages and disadvantages and consider which ones are most important to you. This will help you decide on which franchise is right for you.

66

"LIFE IS WHAT YOU MAKE IT. ALWAYS HAS BEEN, ALWAYS WILL BE."

Eleanor Roosevelt

CHAPTER 6

IS FRANCHISING FOR YOU?

Once you have considered the advantages and disadvantages of franchising and weighed up the pros and cons, it is decision time. Knowing if you are the right sort of person to run a franchise is the first fundamental step. Everybody is unique but there are certain behaviours, motivations and values that are common to successful franchisees. Knowing this can be the difference between success and failure. Take a long, hard look at yourself and weigh up the pros and cons before deciding that franchising is right for you. Some of the pros and some of the cons may be more important to you than others.

ARE YOU RIGHT FOR FRANCHISING?

Ask yourself the following six questions:

1. Am I prepared to follow someone else's system? If you are the type of person who always thinks they are right and finds it difficult to conform, then maybe franchising isn't for you.

2. Am I prepared to take personal responsibility? Do you blame others if things don't always go to plan? You are accountable for your own actions and their consequences.

3. Am I prepared to do whatever it takes to be successful? Building a successful business, whether a franchise or not, requires a great deal of commitment, time and effort. Be prepared to get out of your comfort zone.

4. What am I trying to achieve from franchising and do I have a plan to achieve it?

5. Am I prepared to do self-analysis on a regular basis? Look in the mirror, not only will you see the problem, but you will also see the answer.

6. Have I got the 3D's: Dedication, Determination and Discipline?

When answering the above questions be honest with yourself. It is advisable to write your answers down, as it becomes more of a commitment and they are more likely to embed what you are thinking about.

Based on your answers to these questions, do you still think that franchising is right for you?

If you've made the decision that franchising is right for you – congratulations! You've taken the first step to owning your own business.

CASE STUDY
SUCCESSFUL FRANCHISEE

During the years that I owned Sameday UK I encountered all types of franchisees from all types of backgrounds. One of the best and most successful was a guy who had been an engineer in the Royal Navy for over 20 years. Because of his background he had the discipline to follow the system, he was punctual, he always wore his uniform and his vans were always clean. He was so determined to succeed that he would spend a couple of hours on a Sunday dropping leaflets through every company door on an industrial estate. He would then spend most of his Mondays on the phone contacting them to make appointments. He would go and meet them and would invariably do business with them. He was an amiable character who knew everything about the service — people buy from people they know, like and trust. That requires some dedication and it paid dividends. As a result, he won the Franchisee of the Year Award.

CASE STUDY
UNSUCCESSFUL FRANCHISEE

At Sameday UK, our busiest day of the week was Friday. We had some big customers like Carlsberg and Punch Taverns and we could be delivering to pubs and clubs until 11 o'clock at night. Therefore a franchisee could earn double the average day on a Friday. We took on a franchisee who gave all the right answers and seemed to tick all the right boxes during the interview process. However, after about three months, the staff informed me that they couldn't contact him after 4pm on a Friday as his phone was switched off. As he lived relatively close to our offices I asked him to come in for a meeting and, after a lot of 'digging', I finally discovered the reason. He did karaoke on a Friday night in his local club and wanted to get home early to have a meal and get ready. This was someone who had just invested a considerable amount of money in the franchise. I don't think I need to tell you what my reaction was and what I said to him. Needless to say, he was a failure as a franchisee and didn't last long.

WHERE DO YOU START?

At this point it is good to make a list of all the things that you will need to do.

Once you have been honest with yourself and if you are willing to take the leap, you will need to think about what exactly you want from your franchise. This will make it easier for you to choose the right franchise. Remember, this new business will take a lot of dedication, determination and discipline and these qualities are so much easier to find and maintain if you are doing something you love doing, something that interests you and something that fits in with your lifestyle and personality.

EXERCISE:

Here are ten questions to ask yourself so that you will be better prepared for the next chapter when you will narrow down the franchise which is right for you:

1. **What type of franchise am I looking for?** There are over 900 franchise brands in the UK covering 80 business sectors, so there is a lot to choose from. Would you prefer service or retail, 24 hour or 9-5, or something that already interests you or you are already experienced in the field, e.g. photography, fitness etc. (more on this in the next chapter).

2. **How much can I afford to invest?** Like any new business venture, when starting a franchise there is a certain amount of risk involved. Many franchisors have a low initial franchise fee but the total investment can be huge due to the cost of equipment and fit out costs. This is typical in the coffee shop and fast food market.

3. **What is the likely Return on Investment (ROI)?** This will differ substantially from one franchise to another. Most new businesses go through a start-up phase where they lose money for a while, then break even and ultimately become profitable. The curve of this initial growth phase is usually fairly sharp in the beginning, and then the business stabilizes and begins experiencing a more normal growth rate as it matures. For an average business, this process takes about two to three years. For this reason, when we look at the monetary return for a franchise, we usually look at what our income expectations are based on the business being in its third year of operation.

   When evaluating what is a reasonable return in a franchise, begin by looking at the return on invested capital. Since starting any business is considered a relatively risky investment, you should be able to earn a very good return on your invested capital, let's say in the region of 15%.

   Calculating a reasonable return on your investment of time is more difficult because of the variables involved. Start by asking yourself what your time is worth in general terms. The analysis gets a bit more complicated, though, when you factor in lifestyle changes that can come with owning your own business. For example, let's say that the business will provide you with a great deal of flexibility or that it doesn't require any travel. That may mean that you'll never again miss your child's birthday party or that you'll finally be able to coach a soccer team like you've always wanted.

As another example, let's say that the £30,000 job you currently have involves doing tasks every day that you really dislike, or that you've got a boss that you can't stand working for. Getting away from those factors and into a situation where they don't apply may have a great deal of non-monetary value to you. These types of 'soft' factors are undoubtedly important to consider, but they are difficult to quantify with a fixed monetary value that we can use to compute a return on investment.

4. **How long before I make a profit?** Do your homework before deciding if a franchise is worth the investment. Some franchises are profitable in the first few months while others are a long-term investment. Consider the cash flow position relating to your current situation. Do you need to make money from day one to pay the bills or have you sufficient funds to ride any bad periods?

5. **Should I use my current bank or approach another?** In general, the banks look favourably on franchising and will often lend up to 70% of the total investment on a well-established franchise brand. With newer franchises, it is generally 50-50. Some of the major banks have large franchise departments, notably NatWest and HSBC.

6. **Where will I find a good franchise solicitor?** The BFA has a list of affiliated franchise solicitors and it is advisable to use one to check any franchise agreements. General solicitors may be cheaper, but do they know what to look for? You get what you pay for. Remember it is a long-term commitment and hopefully everything will be fine, but you never know!

7. **Is it worth seeking advice from a franchise consultant?** The simple answer is Yes, but make sure that it is one that has been there and done it, someone who has worn the tee shirt.

8. **What timeframe am I looking at?** How soon do I want to start? Are there things I need to put in place first – business or personal? Will the franchise I choose be influenced by the seasons? How many hours do I want to work and how do I want to work? Some franchises can mean very long hours and with some you are on your feet all day. It is worth giving it some thought.

9. **Do I want to work weekends or Bank Holidays?** If you don't want to work weekends it is pointless buying a franchise that requires you to do so. Even if you are buying a franchise as an investment and not working in it yourself on a day to day basis you can still encounter problems — staff not turning in and equipment breaking down are just a couple.

 **ACTIVITY:**

Draw up a plan of action.

	Answer	Action Required	By When?
The main factors I am looking for in my franchise, e.g. type (retail vs service), working hours, lifestyle.			
How much can I afford to invest?			

	Answer	Action Required	By When?
What sort of ROI do I want?			
How soon do I want/need to profit from my investment?			
Do I need to approach my current bank for investment? Are they the right bank for my franchise?			
Should I approach other banks? Make a list and enquire about rates.			

	Answer	Action Required	By When?
Make a list of some BFA approved franchise solicitors and investigate them.			
Note down some franchise consultants and investigate them.			
When do I want to start?			

"THE STARTING POINT OF ALL ACHIEVEMENT IS DESIRE."

Napolean Hill

CHAPTER 7

WHAT TYPE OF FRANCHISE ARE YOU LOOKING FOR?

You've made the decision that franchising is right for you so you've taken the first step to owning your own business. Next comes the even more difficult part — which franchise should you invest in?

Buying a franchise is a HUGE investment, so choosing the right one for you is incredibly important. Here are ten top tips on how you should do it.

CHOOSING THE RIGHT FRANCHISE FOR YOU.

Step 1: Know yourself.

The best place to start is with you. Determine exactly what results you want to accomplish in business. To help, complete a personal inventory of your strengths and weaknesses and calculate the amount of financial resources you have available to start a business.

Step 2: What can you afford?

The reality is when buying a franchise, you must first consider what you can actually afford. Within franchising there is a business model to fit every budget, starting from an initial investment of as little as £495 to over £100,000. You are likely to still have a number of choices whatever your budget.

Think about how much you are able to invest, how much liquid cash you have and how much you would be willing to borrow. While you're working to set up and establish your business, chances are it won't be making a profit — so make sure you consider your working capital requirements. One of the main reasons that 45% of new businesses fail in the first year of trading is poor cash flow, they run out of cash. The number of new franchisees failing is a lot less due to the fact that they are buying into an established brand and also that reputable franchisors will want to see evidence that a new franchisee has sufficient resources to sustain the business through the early stages. You may be tempted by the return on investment offered by some of the brands but is it worth it if all you are doing is working hard to pay back loans for ten years or more.

We've previously mentioned that banks are more likely to lend to an individual purchasing a franchise than someone starting their own stand-alone business. A number of banks, such as HSBC and NatWest, have teams that specialise in franchise loans. Speak to them, talk about the options available to you — it may make a huge difference in your final choice. Most banks say they will lend up to 75% for a franchise but the reality is normally 50% unless you are buying into a major brand. This can often say something about the franchise opportunity so take note.

Step 3: Overview of the Franchise Market.

There are over 900 franchise operations in the UK, covering nearly every business sector that you can think of. There are B2B, B2C, lifestyle, man and a van, and big investment franchises. Want to own a hair salon? There's a franchise for that. A homecare business? There's franchises for that too. An oven cleaning company? Yes — there are franchise opportunities in that! So how do you decide? Knowing what you want from a business is a good point of reference.

First have a look at some of the franchise recruitment websites like Franchise Direct and Franchise UK. This will give you an overall picture of the large number and types of franchise that are available.

You may even discover something that you have never even thought of or considered. Have a look at the franchise magazines, they are full of interesting articles and case studies of franchisees. Attend the various franchise exhibitions and seminars to get a feel for the industry. You will not only meet franchisors but franchise consultants and finance providers too. Google 'franchises' in a particular sector to see what comes up.

Step 4: Narrow down the search.

At this stage, most people are looking at between six and ten franchises. What interests you and what you enjoy doing? Also have a think about what you really wouldn't like to do and cross if off the list. Some franchises require certain skill sets, qualifications, or experience, while some need more personal qualities. Let's be realistic, you shouldn't buy a franchise that involves teaching children to swim if you can't swim! Having said that, you may be looking for a management or investment franchise where you employ others to carry out the day to day operation. You only live once and this will be a big part of your life so it is pointless doing something that you don't enjoy, even if it earns you a good income.

Step 5: Research the market.

Once you have chosen the sector that you want to be in and the level of investment, research the market. What do you know about it? Is it growing, steady or declining? Then choose three or four franchises that fit the profile. Speak to professionals. Know what you're getting in to.

Step 6: Research the franchise.

Many potential franchisees start off by looking on one of the franchise recruitment websites. They look at various sectors that are appealing and within their price range. They will send for a prospectus for as many as ten franchises and once they have researched them they will focus in on three franchises to compare and then make the final decision. It's a great way of finding the franchisor that's right for you.

When comparing franchises, make sure you have as much information as possible; you can never have enough. Attend an exhibition or a discovery day, request a prospectus, make phone calls, or arrange a meeting. It's all about due diligence. Take time to carefully review the franchise disclosure document. In addition to earnings claims and financial statements, consider any litigation or bankruptcy information in the document. If you're investing any sum of money, you need to know as much as possible. Ask about the training, the support offered, who you will be dealing with, the ongoing fees, and the business model. Speak to existing franchisees at different levels of development. Ask the franchisor about themselves — what experience do they have? How has the business grown? How many franchisees have been successful or, in fact, unsuccessful? Verify values and culture. Spend time with the employees of the franchise company if possible to make sure they have the same values and priorities as you do.

TOP 10 QUESTIONS TO ASK A FRANCHISOR

1. ABC is clearly successful and growing significantly. What do you attribute this success to considering the high level of competition within your sector?
2. What type of person is an ideal franchisee and flourishes with an ABC franchise?
3. What do you think are the main benefits of being an ABC franchisee?
4. Can you give me more information about the finances — your start-up costs, franchise fee, ongoing management fees, cash flow and profit and loss forecasts.
5. How long will it take me to recoup my investment?
6. How much training do you provide, what does it involve and is it on-going?
7. How long have you been franchising and how many franchised outlets are you running at the moment?
8. Who has been your most successful franchisee to date and what have they achieved?
9. Have you had any franchisees fail?
10. Can I speak to your existing franchisees?

A good franchisor will be transparent, they will tell you everything you need to know. If a franchisor appears to be hiding something, it's unlikely it's anything good. However, the process is two-way. You should be assessed for your understanding of the business, franchising in general and whether you fit the model. If it is not a lengthy and slightly difficult process alarm bells should start ringing. A poor franchisor will just see your cheque and take your money. Good franchisors will be focussed on what you can deliver and how you can help to grow the business. It is pointless to compromise the business for short term gain.

Step 7. Talk to existing franchisees.

This is one of the best ways to gauge what being a franchisee will be like. Talk to as many as you can and ask them the following questions:

- Are you profitable and making money?
- Have you recovered your investment?
- Can you verify the company's earning claims?
- What training and support is provided?
- Have there been any unexpected costs or surprises?
- Has the franchisor managed to resolve any disputes fairly?
- How would you describe your relationship with the franchisor?

The answers to these questions should give you a very good insight into whether the franchise is right for you, but be mindful of the possible motivations in what they tell you.

Step 8: Get advice.

Whether it be a friend, family member, bank, solicitor, consultant or any other individual — receiving independent advice from an outside party can be a huge benefit and talking about it with someone else helps you to clarify your thoughts.

Step 9: Take your time.

Buying a franchise is probably one of the biggest investments you'll ever make. Take your time and make sure you're confident with your decision. A franchise is a big commitment; you shouldn't be pressured into making a decision. One doubt is a doubt too many!

Step 10: Take calculated risks.

Successful franchisees aren't typically gamblers — they want any risk they take to be as small and carefully controlled as possible. But once you have decided on the right franchise for you give it 100% commitment to achieve success.

ESTABLISHED FRANCHISES V EARLY FRANCHISES

Should You Be the First Franchisee?

Yes, but only if your gut instinct (and your due diligence) says so.

When carrying out due diligence on a franchise opportunity, one of the best ways is to talk to existing or former franchisees. They will be able to give you their opinions on every aspect of the business and an honest assessment.

However, this is not always possible, particularly if you are the first, or one of the first. In this instance, you need to be satisfied that the company is well established and has run a successful pilot operation. Check that they have used advisors with a proven track record in franchising. The franchisor should be able to answer all the basic questions about their franchise systems and finances. If they can't or seem reluctant to do so, stay clear.

Every franchise system has a first franchisee. You can call this person the pioneer, the guinea pig or the ground breaker, but it is still someone who is risking their money and investing with the hope of building a successful business. As important as success is to the first franchisee, it is even more important to the franchisor, as the future growth of the company will depend to a large extent on the results and validation of the first franchisee.

As a first franchisee, you have to be a very special type of person. You must be much more accepting of risk than a normal investor. Bold and brave, you should also be the type of person who's willing to deal with a more fluid situation, where changing and adapting to unforeseen circumstances is a welcome part of business development. The first franchisee is usually a true entrepreneur and, much more so than later franchisees, is a partner with the franchise company in the development of the franchise system.

In many ways, being the first franchisee is comparable to being a first child. The good thing about being first is all the extra attention that normally comes with the position. The challenging thing is that the first child has to break the ice on every little thing. This makes it much easier for the children that come later, but it's sometimes a real pain for the first child. They have to effectively train the parents to be reasonable and have realistic expectations, and this is often the same dynamic at play between the franchise company and the first franchisee.

There are some key factors to making sure you're successful as a first franchisee. The big three are:

1. Be the right person.

It's essential for both you and the franchise company to understand the unique role that the first franchisee plays. The first franchisee is a person who's comfortable with the uncertainty involved in being the icebreaker for a system. The good news is that you're undoubtedly going to receive a great deal of extra support from the senior staff of the franchise company. The bad news is that you're going to represent a learning environment for the franchise, and you need to be able to accept that role.

2. Have realistic expectations.

No matter how well the franchise prototype or pilot operations have performed, it's going to be different running the first franchise unit. You aren't going to understand everything about the business, and it is inevitable that both you and the franchisor are going to learn by making some mistakes. There must be a fair amount of open and frank communication about what areas of the business are set in stone, and what areas will involve testing and learning as you build your business.

3. Get the right deal.

The reality is that the franchisor is going to be using you as a learning tool to a certain extent, so both sides need to be reasonable about who should pay what in terms of training and development. Though the support level given to the first franchisee is typically much more significant than for later franchisees, other value factors, such as the system documentation, are probably not going to be nearly as well defined or developed as they will be later. When negotiating the franchise agreement and other financial considerations, you should address these factors. Both you and the franchisor must feel that the deal is fair and proper.

What are some advantages and disadvantages for you being the first franchisee?

You can receive a lot of glory and recognition for your part in advancing the franchise system, but there are certainly trade-offs. You won't have other franchisees to consult with that have already travelled the path before you. You'll have lots of support and assistance, but the support won't be tested and proven on others, so mistakes are going to be made. You will also have to make your decision to get involved with the franchise without the benefit or assurance provided by an existing system with a number of successful franchisees, and that increases the risk of getting involved. Banks can also look less favourably on first franchisees, especially if it isn't a well-established brand.

So, if you're contemplating becoming a first franchisee, you should carefully consider all the special traits and responsibilities of this role, and make sure that you see yourself as representing a learning environment for the franchise, and you need to be comfortable with that role.

The benefits of being the first franchisee can be summarised in three words — Ground Floor Opportunity. However, being a pioneer in a new system often means being a guinea pig as well and involves a certain amount of risk.

Being the first means that you are closer to the owner of the business and will probably be able to exert your influence and ideas as the network develops, being able to be a part of the decision-making process and being able to contribute to determining the direction of the franchise and helping to create something with huge potential as the brand grows.

One of the disadvantages is that creating a brand through franchising doesn't happen overnight and it can be frustrating in the early days as you want everything to happen quickly. Systems and methods will change as the business evolves and you need to be prepared to embrace these.

Looking at being the first from a financial point of view could also have benefits as in the early days franchise fees are often lower than with an established franchise.

Whatever franchise you are considering, the best piece of advice is to do due diligence on every aspect of the business. Meet and talk to as many people involved as you can, look at the track record to date, look at past business practices, check references, and listen to your gut instincts.

One of the keys to success in franchising is the relationship between the franchisor and the franchisee. If someone is trying to sell too hard, or it seems too good to be true, it probably is. If your interest is flagging, then it probably isn't for you. On the other hand, if you are getting excited about the business, it's a good sign that you are on the right path. One of the most important things in a relationship is the ability to communicate, and that's what I mean by listen to your gut instincts. If you sit back and listen and don't get caught up in the excitement, you'll know.

SHOULD YOU BE THE FIRST FRANCHISEE?

It took over a year for one of my clients to recruit their first franchisee. It took so long for a variety of reasons. Firstly, as a Sweet Shop & Party Venue, they operate in a relatively niche market; secondly, they rejected a couple of interested prospects who they felt weren't right for their business; and thirdly, some prospects didn't want to risk being the first franchise.

Interestingly, two prospects set up almost identical businesses on their own and in fairly close proximity. Both failed and closed down within 12 months of opening, mainly because they had no experience but still thought they could do it themselves. The first franchisee had a very successful launch and is delighted with the progress that they have made and will be a great recommendation for future franchise prospects. Although they had no previous experience in this type of business, they were prepared to listen and learn, both from the owners and myself, and were willing to take a risk.

Sometimes it pays to be first!

 **EXERCISE:**

Ask yourself the following questions:

What type of franchise am I looking for?

Is it worth taking the risk with a new franchise?

 **ACTIVITY:**

Research the available franchises then list between 6-10 which will be on your long list:

1.

2.

3.

4.

5.

6.

7.

8.

9.

10.

Everyone is different and has different circumstances. Write down any major concerns that you have and use them to help narrow down your search. Which concerns can be dealt with? Are there any outstanding concerns? If so, who can help you with them?

Once you have sent off for prospectuses from your long list of franchisors, research them and decide on your short list of no more than three:

1.

2.

3.

"HAPPINESS IS THE KEY TO SUCCESS. IF YOU LOVE WHAT YOU ARE DOING, YOU WILL BE SUCCESSFUL."

Albert Schweitzer

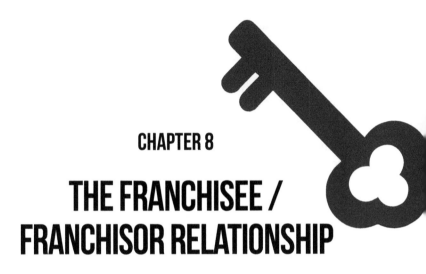

CHAPTER 8

THE FRANCHISEE / FRANCHISOR RELATIONSHIP

There is no question that one of the main keys to the success of a franchise is the relationship between the franchisee and the franchisor. A strong and effective business relationship is critical to the success of both businesses and the franchise system overall.

THE 7 KEY CHARACTERISTICS OF A SUCCESSFUL FRANCHISE SYSTEM:

Alignment: In a franchise system, consistency in values, ethics and behaviours is critical, and helps define the system. For full alignment, these behaviours need to extend beyond the franchise system to other business relationships, such as accountants and suppliers.

Accountability and Responsibility: Franchise partners need to agree and be clear on their respective obligations and responsibilities, and be accountable to them at all times.

Clear, written agreements and contracts can avoid uncertainty and miss-matched expectations. Make sure you read and understand contracts and agreements before you sign them, and that you can meet your obligations. Once signed, contracts are binding and enforceable.

Where problems do arise, be prepared to inform the other party immediately to attempt to work collaboratively to address the problem. Be accountable for your mistakes as well as your successes.

Commitment: Commitment is necessary to build a long-term business relationship as it provides a solid basis for trust between parties. Successful relationships are built and flourish by an investment in effort. Commitment is about focusing on common, long-term goals and intentions rather than one-off transactions or short-term goals. Build trust by delivering on promises and communicating intentions openly and honestly.

Communication: Communications must be clear, frequent, and transparent to ensure that everyone fully understands the other's position, obligations are met and any issues or problems are raised early. Poor communication is one of the most common reasons for a breakdown in relationships. Franchisors and franchisees need to communicate with each other in a way that is relevant, comprehensive and timely.

Mutual Interest: The mutual interest of franchisee and franchisor is a key characteristic of a franchise relationship. Seek to understand each other's business expectations and points of view and identify where mutual interests can be pursued for profitable and sustainable outcomes. Adopt a collaborative approach to problem solving to achieve common interests.

Pre-agreed dispute resolution: All business relationships are likely to have a dispute at one time or another. Agreeing on dispute resolution procedures at the start of a business relationship can be critical in addressing disputes quickly and effectively when they arise, and enabling the business relationship to continue.

Litigation of commercial disputes should be a last resort. It is costly, time consuming, destroys the business relationship and usually has a winner and a loser. Including low cost dispute resolution procedures such as mediation in your agreements and contracts can avoid matters unnecessarily escalating to litigation.

Professional Conduct: Conducting yourself professionally should be a prerequisite for any business relationship. This includes both the way you personally interact with the other business person, as well as how you go about your business. Many of the behaviours associated with professional conduct are common sense. Treat others as you would expect them to treat you. Don't promise what you can't deliver. Meet your obligations.

Show professional business conduct by having a robust, well-researched business plan, with input from relevant professional advisers. Join an industry association, chamber of commerce or other body to keep up to date with good business practice, obtain information relevant to your business, and to benefit from the networking opportunities presented.

MANAGING THE FRANCHISOR/FRANCHISEE RELATIONSHIP.

The quality of the franchise relationship is affected by a number of factors, but effective communication is critical in ensuring shared values and, therefore, a relationship characterized by trust and commitment.

The franchisor/franchisee relationship is often compared to a marriage. The franchisor and the franchise are in partnership together, sharing a common purpose and, while there is some merit in this analogy, my feeling is that a marriage is not what the franchisor/franchisee relationship should be.

When we think of marriage, we think of partners in a joint venture relationship with relatively equal footing. Like a joint venture, marriage often starts off with a few negotiations which tend to be on-going: Who empties the bins?, Who does the washing?, and the more serious issues regarding finance. Because each joint venture is unique, all of these issues are subject to negotiation.

With joint venture partners, one of the major concerns that 'spouses' have is how the finances are handled, who does the accounting and where the money goes. On a one-off basis, this is relatively easy to monitor, but on a large scale it can be a big problem. When things go wrong and a joint venture partner or spouse cheats on you, it can become a battle among equals in a divorce court.

As a franchisor, you have the right and obligation to enforce systems and standards, while your franchisees often see themselves as an independent business with the ability to call their own shots – which they are not. Although the relationship is contractual in nature, if a franchisor is ever forced to bring out the franchise agreement, the franchise is already in jeopardy.

Unlike joint ventures and partnerships, franchising is much more like the relationship between a parent and a child. Like the child, the franchisee will go through a variety of growth phases throughout their life.

New franchisees are like babies, they need cuddles and hugs, and they need as much help and support as they can get. As they develop they are still very much dependent on their parents (the franchisor), relying on them for the education, learning and training that will equip them to survive in the world. As they grow older they become less dependent and start to get given some leeway, being allowed to play out with their mates or go to the shop on their own. As they reach the teenage years they often become rebellious, and sometimes moody, pushing and testing the boundaries of the relationship, trying to change or influence the system that has been set out for them, and perhaps breaking some rules. But they still live in their 'parent's' house, and what their parent says goes. It is simply a matter of how forceful the franchisor is and where they draw the line.

Dealing directly with a franchisor who started the company and developed the franchise can be different from dealing with an area manager, who themselves want to be seen delivering for their bosses. Some area managers will want to do things their way and maybe put a different slant on things which can affect the relationship and cause things to go wrong.

What do you do when you love the business and the franchise but your relationship with the area manager is not good or they are not performing in accordance with their duties? In the event of any dispute, both parties should refer the matter to the franchisor, who would be entitled to arbitrate the dispute. The franchisee should abide by any decision made by the franchisor and should comply with any direction given by the franchisor for the resolution of such a dispute.

WHAT IS A GOOD PARENT/FRANCHISOR?

Over the years I have seen many kids go off the rails because their parents let them do whatever they wanted, with no discipline or guidance. Often other kids envy them at first, but when the ones who had lenient parents end up in court or, worse still, in a detention centre, they are thankful for the way that their own parents brought them up. Sometimes being a great parent means you cannot always be a good friend.

Likewise, a franchisor needs to start by establishing the boundaries of the relationship. It is important that the franchisee understands that the franchisor's first role is to protect the system and the brand, so that all franchisees can grow successfully. This involves discipline and the franchisor needs to clearly communicate the rules and the intention to enforce them from the start.

However, it is important to understand that discipline cannot be meted out in the same way as you did when you owned all your own operations outright. Giving franchisees the "It's my way or the highway" speech will quickly alienate franchisees, and that is the first step to trouble.

Franchisees are business owners and, as such, should be treated with respect, and communicated with in a professional manner. Long-standing established franchises tend to be very rigid — and why shouldn't they be if they are so successful? — but most franchisors are open to ideas and suggestions. Most franchisees like their opinions to be heard and a good franchisor will consider everything and will give clear explanations as to why decisions have been made and about the direction they are going.

DIFFERENT TYPES OF FRANCHISOR

In franchising, you are going to encounter a number of different types of franchisor. Each of them will have their own processes, their own quirky ways, and their own mentalities and, if you want to survive, you're going to need to learn how to deal with all of them.

These are seven of the most common types of franchisor that you will meet:

Hands-on

The hands-on franchisor will generally be involved in the day to day running of the franchised business and will be there to answer any questions that you may have. This doesn't always mean that they want to be your friend. Some will always greet you with a friendly disposition while, for others, it will be strictly business.

Hands-off

The hands-off franchisor takes pride in giving franchisees freedom and flexibility — maybe a little too much at times. They will probably give you limited direction and won't interfere much. They believe that all franchisees will be self-motivated and will do their best with minimal interference. This can be empowering but can also create uncertainty. If your franchisor falls into this category, know that communication is going to be key; if you need help, you're going to have to ask for it. If something's unclear, you'll need to voice your opinion, otherwise you'll be left on your own to deal with it.

The Micromanager

Most micromanagers are born out of internal anxieties and can be difficult to deal with. They are sticklers for details and are always telling you what to do and how to do it. You can voice your opinion, but the micromanager is unlikely to change. Instead, it's better to keep your distance for the tasks you care most about, give feedback, and try to build more trust.

The Power Tripper

The power tripper is often a 'control freak' and may fall into any one of a number of categories. They may be desperate to build the franchise into a national brand at whatever cost. They may only be focused on how they are seen in the eyes of the franchise wold. They may be self-centred and just like the feeling of having power over others. In any case, they can be domineering and inflexible, and may impose strict rules and regulations on you. This can be a challenging position for many, but you can deal with it by making compromises where you can, and communicating openly about how this style affects your ability to grow the franchise.

The Buddy

The buddy wants to be your friend and will always greet you with a cheery disposition. They will be soft when it comes to feedback or advice, and won't set strict criteria. On one hand, you'll get more flexibility in your actions and the way you operate the franchise, but on the other, you will have less constructive criticism on which to build your franchise. In this situation, you will have to ask for feedback directly, and you may need to have the discipline to set the directives, limits and goals for yourself.

The Apathetic

The apathetic franchisor shares some similarities with the hands-off franchisor, but is somewhat more destructive. Whereas the hands-off boss attempts to empower franchisees by giving them more freedom and less interference, the apathetic boss truly doesn't care. They will be hard to communicate with and indifferent to your successes or failures. If you're the type who thrives on feedback, this will be difficult for you. The best approach is to gather feedback however you can from members of the head office team or other franchisees, and focus on your own position.

The Balanced

The balanced franchisor is the rarest type of franchisor, because they embody so many different qualities which keeps them reasonably balanced. They give you flexibility without alienating you, are approachable without crossing the professional line, and will change their mind without losing focus on their original objectives. If you end up working for a balanced franchisor, count yourself lucky!

There are two points that I would like to make about this list. The first is that no one type of boss is inherently 'bad' or 'good'. Yes, it may be frustrating to keep up with a power tripper, or annoying to deal with a micromanager, but there are some advantages to all of these styles that you may not see immediately, and it doesn't mean that they are bad franchisors or indeed bad human beings. Second, this is a list of archetypes. Every franchisor you meet will be unique, with their own set of strengths and weaknesses. Some may fall into several categories, others won't fall into any. This is just a guide to help you navigate some of the most common, and most challenging styles of franchisors out there.

Actually, I do have one more point to make. You have a responsibility as a franchisee to ensure that the relationship works. Therefore, you also have to be honest with yourself and understand your own personality. What are you doing to help or hinder the situation? Sometimes it is six of one and half a dozen of the other!

EFFECTIVE COMMUNICATION IS KEY

The key to a good franchisor/franchisee relationship starts with communication, and that means more than the monthly newsletter, or the occasional field visit from the area manager.

In today's technological world, it is very tempting to rely on the internet for all our communication, but in franchising that would be a big mistake. How often have we seen well-intentioned e-mails or texts get misinterpreted, give the wrong message and cause an uproar?

Relationships are built on dialogue, which should be encouraged. A good franchisor will create multiple streams for two-way communication such as weekly calls, regular visits, regional meetings, access to senior staff and annual events.

To be effective, communication needs to be open and honest, and the key to a long-term sustainable relationship is trust.

Lastly, franchisors need to genuinely care about the success of their franchisees. Good franchisee relationships start with a franchisor that is committed to the success of the franchisees, not just the franchise. If the franchisees do not sense that commitment the relationship can quickly deteriorate. If, on the other hand, franchisees can see that the franchisor is breaking their back to help them achieve their success, there is almost nothing they won't do for them.

FRANCHISEE TRAITS

Just like with franchisors, there are also many different types of franchisee, with different reasons for being in business and what they want to achieve. As stated earlier, the franchisee has as much responsibility to ensure an effective relationship as the franchisor. Below is a table highlighting some of the most common traits.

Franchisee Behaviour

Good Behaviour	Bad Behaviour
Following the format religiously	Not following the format
Keeping in regular contact	Failing to communicate
Giving 100% effort	Playing at it / indifferent
Taking responsibility	Blaming everyone else

Good Behaviour	Bad Behaviour
Suggesting new ideas	Little or no initiative
Helping other franchisees	No co-operation
Flexible	No flexibility
Accepting constructive criticism	Reacting badly to criticism

CASE STUDY:
FOLLOW THE FORMAT

I was once asked for some advice by a franchisor that was in the early stages of development and is now an established brand operating in several countries. They are a business consultancy franchise and their method of franchisees attracting clients is for them to present talks and seminars at business networking events. This was a proven method of attracting new clients. They had signed up a new franchisee in Leeds who had been with them for six months and hadn't done a single talk or seminar but was complaining that he had no business. He had obviously chosen the wrong type of franchise and, needless to say, he didn't last long. There was no legal action as he was clearly in breach of the agreement.

WHAT DO YOU DO IF IT'S NOT WORKING?

In any relationship, there will invariably be issues from time to time and how you deal with them will influence the outcome.

As a franchisee, your first course of action should be to discuss it with the franchisor and, if possible, come up with an amicable solution.

Depending on the nature of the issue, it may also be wise to discuss it with other franchisees, in particular established ones who have been in the network for a while. Most aspects will be covered in the Operations Manual or the Franchise Agreement.

If it cannot be resolved in this way, the next step should be to talk to a recognised franchise consultant and get some advice.

The last step would be to take legal advice from a BFA-approved solicitor. This should always be a last resort as it can be expensive and usually there is only one winner.

It could be that there are no real issues relating to the franchise system, just that it is not working for you, you are not enjoying it or you are not making enough money.

If it really isn't working for you, there are a number of options:

1. You can put the franchise up for sale. You have invested in the franchise with the intention of building a successful business that will produce a good return on investment, but if it is not working it makes sense to move on. Most franchise agreements give you the right to sell your franchise but there will be certain conditions which can vary from one franchise to the other:

   For example, not to sell the franchisee's business without the prior written consent of the franchisor. The franchisor should not unreasonably withhold the right to sell. Also, the franchisor must be satisfied that the proposed purchaser meets the franchisor's finance and management criteria required to run the business and the criteria applicable to new operators. Most franchise agreements will cover these points but not all.

   Another reason why you should have a franchise agreement checked by an approved solicitor before committing to buy a franchise in the first place.

2. You can put someone else in to run it for you. Again, there may be conditions in the franchise agreement relating to this.

3. You can terminate your agreement and walk away from it.

LEGAL ASPECTS

General Overview

Once you have decided that franchising is right for you, and you have found the one that you want to invest in, it is imperative that you get the legalities right. Franchising can be a profitable and rewarding business model but buying into a franchise is a long-term commitment that comes with obligations and liabilities.

A professional and reputable franchise will have a solid legal pack in place to support and protect its proposition and brand. The legal pack will normally consist of three separate documents: the Confidentiality Agreement, the Financial Disclosure Document and the Franchise Agreement. The first two tend to follow a standard format but the Franchise Agreement needs to be a bespoke document, tailor-made to suit the franchise, as no two franchise businesses are the same.

The Confidentiality Agreement

This is often referred to has a non-disclosure agreement and will usually be the first legal document that a franchisor will give you and ask you to sign. You will have already received a prospectus or an information pack and reviewed all the other information available to the public, but you will need to sign this before receiving any more information.

The Deposit Agreement

Most franchisors ask prospective franchisees to pay a deposit at an early stage in the recruitment process once the due diligence has been completed. If this is the case, there should be a deposit agreement setting out the terms under which the deposit is taken and what rights it will provide. Franchisors often request that a deposit is paid as a sign of the prospective franchisee's commitment, and to separate the serious applicants from the time wasters.

A deposit agreement should set out what territory is being secured and how long for, as well as how and when any deposit will be refunded if the transaction doesn't complete. From a franchisees' perspective, paying a deposit may secure their chosen territory and give them exclusivity while they carry out further steps before signing the franchise agreement. Before parting with any cash, you should make sure that you fully understand why you are being asked to pay a deposit, and in what circumstances it will be refunded. Once you have decided to proceed and the final stages are reached, the deposit is normally credited against the franchise fee.

The British Franchise Association expects that a deposit should be refundable, less any direct expenses incurred by the franchisor, if the prospective franchisee decides not to go ahead.

The Franchise Agreement

Both parties will be expected to sign a Franchise Agreement. This is a document that should clearly outline the rights and obligations of both the franchisor and the franchisee in line with the industry code of ethics.

As a minimum requirement, the Franchise Agreement should cover the following 20 essential elements:

1. The rights and obligations granted to the franchisor.

2. The rights and obligations granted to the franchisee.

3. The duration of the agreement — which should be long enough for the franchisee to recoup their initial investment.

4. The rights regarding the territory being granted.

5. The goods and/or services to be provided to the franchisee.

6. The fee structure and payment terms by the franchisee.

7. The rights of the franchisee to use the trade name, trade mark, service mark, logo or any other distinctive signs or identification.

8. Ownership of telephone numbers, domain names and social media accounts.

9. The franchisor's on-going obligations in relation to training and supporting the franchisee.

10. The franchisee's on-going obligations in relation to the operation of the method as in the operations manual.

11. Any requirement for the franchisee to have a business plan.

12. Accounting records that must be submitted to the franchisor.

13. Non-compete requirements in relation to the franchisor and other franchisees.

14. The franchisor's right to change the franchise system and adapt to new or different methods.

15. The terms under which the franchisee may sell or transfer the franchised business, and the franchisor's pre-emption rights in this respect.

16. Provisions for termination of the agreement.

17. Provisions upon termination for the franchisee to surrender any tangible and intangible property belonging to the franchisor.

18. Death or incapacity.

19. Termination for breach of agreement.

20. Disclaimers of the franchisor's liability to the franchisee.

Put simply, this is a document that outlines in legal terms how the franchisor/franchisee relationship works with respect to the rights and obligations of both parties.

Ideally the franchise agreement will have been drafted by a BFA-affiliated lawyer and will meet all the necessary requirements. However, it is wise to obtain your own independent legal advice — it is money well spent. You are investing considerable time, energy and money, and it is best to get it right.

Once signed, make sure that you keep copies of all the legal documents in a safe place for future reference. You will then be able to proceed knowing that you have a solid legal framework to support your new business venture.

Negotiating an agreement

The majority of franchise businesses are the result of experience gained from pilot programmes, proven success and a fundamental understanding in particular markets. The important lessons of taking franchisees from start-up to profit-making have been learned, and it is often the case that franchisors will use a contract template so that the terms of a franchise agreement are non-negotiable.

If a franchisor is willing to negotiate substantial parts of a franchise agreement it should be treated as a 'warning sign' and should lead prospective franchisees to question the confidence in the method, systems and the brand.

Having said that, a prospective franchisee should always ask about a franchisor's position with regards to negotiation, and never be afraid to request as much clarification as is necessary on any of the points in the franchise agreement. It is a matter of due diligence.

A key thing to consider in the responses is, 'Does this response protect the franchise system as a whole?' If it does, then the franchisor is doing their job.

One of the best ways to gain clarity on this matter is to talk to current franchisees as well as the franchisor. They will usually highlight any problems that have occurred.

What can go wrong with a franchise agreement?

Most franchise agreements are designed first and foremost to protect the brand and should cover every aspect of the business, giving clear guidance to both parties.

However, things do go wrong from time to time.

BREACH OF AGREEMENT

A well-established franchisor discovered that one of his franchisees was buying supplies from an unauthorised supplier. He was also selling items for cash and not declaring them, both in breach of the franchise agreement. As per the franchise agreement he gave the franchisee the statutory notice to stop doing this and warned him of the consequences. The franchisee ignored the warning and was eventually taken to court.

The franchisor won the case at a cost of £15,000 but didn't receive a penny as the franchisee declared the business insolvent.

CASE STUDY:
FALSE PROMISES

A franchisor was taken to court by two franchisees for breach of agreement and lost.

The franchisor had 'guaranteed' that franchisees would turnover x amount in their first year, which they didn't, and on the financial projections there was no disclaimer.

A very good reason for a franchisor to use a specialist franchise advisor when setting up a franchise.

 **EXERCISE:**

Ask yourself the following questions:

What is my personality type? Are there any aspects of my personality which cause me to clash with my managers?

Am I prepared to collaborate and be accountable?

 **ACTIVITY:**

List the key good parts and bad parts of your personality that might affect your relationship with the franchisor. e.g. I am very disciplined but can be abrasive if things don't go my way.

Can you control the bad parts in a working relationship?

Are there any personality types you find difficult to work with? e.g. someone who you see as 'nit-picking' and always finding fault. How would you change your way of working to cope with them?

"DO WHAT YOU DID AT THE BEGINNING OF A RELATIONSHIP, AND THERE WON'T BE AN END."

Anthony Robbins

CHAPTER 9

HOW ARE YOU GOING TO RUN YOUR BUSINESS?

You could have the best idea in the world, be the most skilled, have lots of energy and determination and yet your business can still be a flop.

It is important to spend time mapping out how you are going to run your business before you start. Even when your business has been running for a few months, it is always beneficial to spend some time on how you run your business as it evolves.

The majority of new start-up businesses are the result of one person's idea which they then develop and hopefully grow successfully. In the early days that person may be the only one working in the business before they decide to employ staff, or they may outsource certain elements such as finance, human resources, health & safety, or social media. They do everything themselves, usually spending long hours working in the business, which can sometimes affect their family life and their health.

However, as we know, approximately 45% of all new businesses fail within 18 months of starting up, and around 85% don't survive beyond 5 years. Statistically, only 4% of business owners ever reach the £1m mark, and only 10% of those (that's 0.4% of all business owners) ever reach the £10m mark.

Starting a business requires no formal education or qualification, and an entrepreneur is likely to strike out on their own armed with little else than a great idea, passion and a set of skills from their previous life that may or may not be relevant to the business they intend to build.

The first year of the life of this fledgling business is the most critical. During this time, the rookie entrepreneur is focused on survival, their goals tend to be modest, and their successes are rarely outstanding. But while that may be an acceptable beginning for some, the high failure rate, especially within 5 years, is an issue. The trouble is, what allows many entrepreneurs to run a successful small business simply cannot support larger teams and issues; further improvement and growth is too complex for them to handle and pursue. They've hit a complexity ceiling.

Donald Rumsfeld and NASA before him originated the concept of the importance of acknowledging and planning for what we don't know. What an entrepreneur doesn't know, and how they go about identifying and filling that knowledge gap is what separates a £1m-plus turnover business from an also-ran.

THE NUMBER GAME

Whatever the product, whatever the market, every business needs to master communication. While most entrepreneurs understand this, what many fail to learn (or forget) is that businesses all over the world speak the same language – numbers.

Numbers relating to Sales, Cash Flow, Profit, Receivables, Assets, Average Sales Value, Conversion Rate, Equity and ROI. A successful business person must not only understand these numbers, they must be able to leverage them for every decision made in their business.

In marketing, sales, team management and leadership there are key metrics to average, estimate and measure in order to evaluate the probability of effects and to justify decisions and take calculated risks that will lead to sustainable growth.

Understanding this language is essential at every stage of business, but it becomes vital as a business starts growing in size and complexity. And among the vital things an entrepreneur must grasp is that understanding numbers helps keep track of growth systematically, without having to do everything themselves, and that the relative importance of running their business as a business increases as they lose the ability to be personally involved in every activity the business undertakes.

IN/ON/OUT

There is a lot to be said for the in/on/out approach to running a business, and although it can be difficult in the early days it usually is beneficial. Some entrepreneurs will just embrace the in/out version first. That means they will work in the day to day running of the business 50% of the time and will spend the other 50% working on the strategy and how to improve the business. As it develops and grows they may adopt the in/on/out approach, which means they will spend 30% of their time working in the business, 30% on their business and 30% outside their business.

Working outside the business could involve many things and will be different for each individual. It could involve looking at new ideas, attending exhibitions and seminars, going to networking meetings, or simply spending more time with other business people, family and friends.

DOWNTIME

The failure of a business is often caused by entrepreneurs and new business owners working so hard at their business that they forget how to live their life. Family, health, friendships and wellbeing all suffer as a consequence.

CASE STUDY
MY FIRST BUSINESS

I remember when I started my first business, I was 27 at the time and worked long hours. I was passionate about football and the only time that I wasn't thinking about my business was when I was on the football field on a Saturday afternoon. It didn't get any easier as the business grew, and as I took on staff, in some ways it got harder. After five years of slogging away without a holiday I needed a break. I was sitting in my office early one evening surrounded by paperwork and had had enough. I tipped my desk over, got up and went to the pub where most of my football friends were. I went to the bar and announced, "I am going on holiday if anyone wants to come." My best friend Vinnie asked me when I was going, to which I replied, "As soon as I can get a ticket." Three days later we were in Benidorm, my first holiday abroad, and we had a fantastic time. It didn't affect the business and made me realise that you need to take time out when building a business, otherwise what's the point?

WHAT WILL BE YOUR STYLE?

So, before you take the plunge ask yourself the following questions.

Hands on or Hands off?

Are you going to be hands on, a manager or an investor? As an example, in a retail outlet the franchisee may be working in the shop hands on every day, or they may manage the shop with staff doing all the day to day stuff. They may also be an investor who puts others in to manage and operate the shop. Although most franchisees start with one outlet, it is quite common now for franchisees to own multiple outlets which makes sense from both sides. If a franchisee has been successful with one outlet and wants to grow, it makes sense to buy another one.

Likewise, it makes sense from the franchisor's perspective, as the franchisee has proved themselves and there will be fewer franchisees to deal with. I know franchisees who own over 30 outlets, which means that the franchisor is dealing with one person, not 30.

How am I going to be involved and how much time am I prepared to give?

Do you want to be full-time or part-time? Do you want to work evenings and/or weekends? Are you prepared to spend time on training and self-development? Do you really want to give up your holidays?

These are all things that should be considered seriously before buying a franchise.

There are many franchises now that can be operated on a part-time basis, which is ideal for parents with young families or someone who is not ready to give up their full-time job but wants extra income. It is one of the reasons why there has been a substantial increase in the number of female franchisees over the past few years.

Even if you are a management type franchisee and your franchise operates evenings and weekends with other people staffing your business, there will be times when equipment breaks down and you have to sort it, there will be times when staff go off sick or hand in their notice and leave, and you have to go in and cover for them. So you need to think very carefully about the type of franchise that you want, what it involves and your role in it.

Who is going to help me?

All franchisees need help and guidance along the way and most of it should come from the franchisor. Other successful franchisees in the same network can also be a good source of help and advice. They have been there and worn the tee shirt and will be aware of any pitfalls. You may also have friends, relatives and business associates who are prepared to help and advise you.

You will need an accountant, a solicitor, HR, H&S and insurance consultants and some of these may be recommended by the franchisor. All of these requirements will be covered in your franchise agreement and invariably the onus is on you as the franchisee to provide them. Bear in mind that just because you delegate certain functions, it doesn't mean that you absolve responsibility. You or your company will still be responsible for any actions taken.

You may also need help and support from family and friends which is not directly to do with the business. You may need a bit more support at home in the beginning as your business may take up more of your time. You may have less time for cooking and cleaning and you may have to look at childcare options. You may also need someone to talk to and give you moral support to help you cope with the ups and downs.

How will I celebrate my successes?

I remember speaking to one of Richard Branson's secretaries some years ago and she said, "He celebrates everything possible: birthdays, staff anniversaries, company achievements and milestones." Everyone should celebrate success, no matter how small... I certainly do. How you celebrate your success is down to you; there are many ways. It could be just taking all your team out for a meal or it could be a big event with an awards ceremony. The important thing is that you celebrate success.

When you buy a reputable franchise, you are in effect buying a proven system, a ready-made business, and a lot of the problems of starting your own business from scratch can be avoided. However, you will still have to work hard and follow the business format to be successful.

 **EXERCISE:**

Ask yourself the following questions:

How am I going to run my business?

Who is going to help me?

 **ACTIVITY:**

Write down all the things that that might affect your ability to run the business and answer them honestly. I've given you some examples. e.g. Don't know about cash flow.

Challenges	Action to Face the Challenges
Don't know about finance – cash flow	Talk to an accountant or bank manager
Never done Sales and Marketing	Enrol on a course / buy a book about it
Never run my own business	Buy a book about business
Don't have many contacts	Attend networking meetings
Never recruited staff	Talk to an HR specialist

"A BUSINESS HAS TO BE INVOLVING, IT HAS TO BE FUN, AND IT HAS TO EXERCISE YOUR CREATIVE INSTINCTS."

Richard Branson

CHAPTER 10

BUSINESS PLANNING

RUNNING THE BUSINESS

Some franchises will include specific business planning in their model, with clear steps and guidance, others won't. However, I believe that the process of completing a Business Plan is a fundamental element of running a successful franchise, just like any other business. If you require funding, you will almost certainly have to do a business plan and projections based on the information given to you by the franchisor. It is clearly in your own interests.

The process should be a lot easier with a franchise than with your own start-up business as you are buying into a proven model that will have, or should have, most of the facts and figures. Nevertheless, you are still running your own business and need clear ideas about what you want to achieve and how you are going to achieve it.

A basic business plan should include all of the following:

1. Executive Summary

This is one of the most important parts of your business plan and it should explain the basics of your business so that anyone reading it can understand what the business is about. It should include the key points of your business plan and should be short – no longer than two pages. It should include the following three elements:

✓ **Business Summary:** Explain what the business is about, what you are selling and to whom. Explain what type of business structure you have chosen to be — sole trader, limited company etc., and why you have chosen it. Often, but not always, this is decided by the franchisor and the various options will be stated in the franchise agreement.

✓ **Business Aims:** List three or four goals that you want to achieve through your business. For example, you might want to earn enough money to support your family in a comfortable lifestyle, or enough to enable you to retire, or you may want to have multiple outlets. Your goals should be divided into short term (one year), medium term (three years) and long term (five+ years).

✓ **Financial Summary:** State how much money you need to start the business and explain where you will get it from. Are you contributing yourself, and if not, why not, or are you borrowing from other sources? Outline your financial goals for the first year – what turnover and profit you expect and how much actual cash you will have.

Because it is a summary of your business plan, you should write it last.

2. Elevator Pitch

Sometimes it is difficult to have the right words ready to explain your business to a potential customer. You need to plan how you are going to talk about your business, what you are going to say that it makes it easy for people to understand. You need to explain concisely what your business does, who it is for and what makes it different from the competition.

Your business name is important because it is often the first thing people see on your marketing material, your website, your vehicles, or your premises. Your name helps people to form an impression of what you do, what you stand for and can differentiate you from the competition. You have to live with it, so you need to think about it. What your name says about you and your business and how it influences potential customers.

Straplines are catchy phrases that go with your business name, for example – Sameday UK "Delivered Today". Not all businesses need a strapline and some franchises do and some don't.

Your Elevator Pitch should be a quick two-minute summary of your business. One or two sentences that you choose to tell potential customers when you only have a couple of minutes to make an impression. Your elevator pitch should clearly state what your business does, who is it for, and why it is different. After a little practice, it will become second nature.

Some franchises will already have an elevator pitch and some won't.

3. About You

This section should explain why you have bought the franchise and why you have the ability, experience, and commitment to make it a success. It should also give details of your education, qualifications, training, work experience and hobbies. You should attach a CV for every person involved in the franchise.

4. Products and Services

People reading your business plan may not be familiar with your products or services, so you need to explain everything, even if it seems obvious to you. Ask someone who is not associated with the business to read your description to make sure that they can understand it.

5. Marketing

A well-established franchise will usually have a sales and marketing system in place, often with a manual covering all the different aspects, but again some don't. Marketing can be split into the following three sections:

✓ **Target Market:** Who are your Potential Customers? Describe the type of customers that might buy your products or services? Are they companies or individuals? You need to understand these potential customers so that you can work out how to tell them about your business. Be specific and find out as much information as you can. If they are businesses, what sector are they operating in? If they are individuals, is there an age bracket? Where are they based – local, UK, abroad or all?

✓ **Market Research:** Most of your potential customers will already be using other businesses. You need to research those businesses and their customers. There is no right amount of research, but it is better to research the local market in the area that you will be working in than researching the entire global market. Your research should tell you what your market looks like, how it behaves and what customers expect. There are basically two types of research: desk research and field research. Desk research uses information gathered from books, published statistics and the internet. Field research involves asking potential customers their opinions about your business offering. You can use questionnaires or surveys, and it is one of the best ways of working out if you will be successful.

✓ **Marketing Strategy:** How will you contact your potential customers? Marketing is an activity that attempts to make contact with potential customers and inform them about your business. Good marketing material will grab your potential customer's attention, capture their interest, feed their desire for your product or service and prompt them to find out more and take action. Different marketing methods work best for different companies and a franchisor should already have that knowledge to pass on to franchisees. Below is a list of marketing methods that you could use.
- Word of mouth
- Advertising
- Leaflets, literature and business cards
- Direct marketing
- Exhibitions and trade shows
- Social Media
- Website

Word of mouth: If customers like your business they will often recommend it to others — that's word of mouth marketing. However, it is worth considering how you could encourage them to tell other people, for example, by offering an incentive like a discount or by giving exceptional customer service.

Advertising: There are many ways to advertise your business, for example, in a local paper, a trade magazine, on the internet through your website or social media. A good franchisor will already have chosen the best methods to use and the type of advert, for example, colour and size. They should also advise on the length of an advertising campaign and the cost.

Leaflets, literature and business cards: The franchisor will already have produced some and you should attach them to your business plan. You will usually receive a certain amount as part of the initial package and will re-order as and when required.

Direct marketing: This involves contacting potential customers to directly sell your product or service to them. It can be done by e-mail, on the phone, in a letter, or face-to-face. Again, the franchisor should be able to tell you which methods work the best and which are cost effective.

Exhibitions and trade shows: Some businesses can access large audiences at an exhibition or a trade show. However, exhibiting is expensive and time consuming, so you need to be sure it will be worth the effort. An established franchisor will be able to advise you accordingly.

Social Media: Using social media can be a very effective way of marketing your business. It is mostly free, allows you to put a face to your business and invites a vast network to interact with your activities. As well as Facebook and Twitter, there is Instagram, YouTube and LinkedIn. Which ones you use will be determined by which networking sites are preferred by your target market. A good franchisor will have strict guidelines on the use of social media in order to protect the brand. Some will allow their franchisees to do their own and others will do it all through head office.

Website: Your website is one of the first places that prospective customers will go to for information about your business. Again, this can vary from one franchise to another. Some will have one national site with a list of their franchisees, some will have a landing page for each franchise and others will allow the franchisee to have their own website, as long as it has been approved by the franchisor.

6. Competitor Analysis

A competitor is any business that offers a product or service that is similar to yours. Most businesses often have many competitors, so it is best to focus on those which customers are most likely to buy from instead of you — probably those with the most similar products or services, with the most similar prices and nearest to you. You need to think clearly about your business and how you compare to your competitors. You should then put your thoughts in a SWOT analysis.

7. SWOT Analysis

SWOT stands for Strengths, Weaknesses, Opportunities and Threats. A SWOT analysis will help you to understand all the things that could affect your business, good and bad. If you know what these are, you can work out how to resolve them, or use them to your advantage. Thinking about your weaknesses and what could go wrong is important because it will give you the chance to correct your mistakes before they happen.

Start by making a list of 5 or 6 competitors in your area. You then need to find out who they are, where they are, what they sell, their prices, how big they are and their strengths and weaknesses.

✓ **Strengths** are positive things about your business that will make it stand out against your competitors. These might be specific to your product or service or more general, such as your location.

✓ **Weaknesses** are all the things that could mean you struggle to make your business work. For example, areas that might be affected by your lack of experience or by lack of money. Address each weakness and how you are going to resolve it. You may need more training or investment.

✓ **Opportunities** come in all shapes and sizes and often when you are not expecting them. They often arise because of external factors that you and your competitors can take advantage of, for example, a competitor closing down, changes in the law or market trends. We have all heard of missed opportunities, so don't miss them, take advantage of them.

✓ **Threats** are usually external factors that could affect the performance of your business and your competitors. For example, a large discount shop or a national brand opening up that might take away your customers. You need to be prepared for these and have a plan as to how you will reduce their effect on your business.

8. Unique Selling Point

Your USP is the thing that makes your business different from your competitors. It might be specific to your product or service or it might relate to the way you operate your business. It will most likely be the reason that customers stopped using a competitor and became your customer. Be specific and avoid clichés such as better quality products, better customer service or cheaper products. Think about how you will show your customers that you are the better choice. An established franchise should have a USP in place but, if not, you need to find one.

9. Operations

All franchisors should have a comprehensive Operations Manual that you can use and refer to when needed. It should cover every aspect of the business, no matter how small, and how it works on a day to day basis. It should cover in depth all of the following:
- An introduction to the company and the system
- Pre-Opening procedures
- Daily Operating Procedures
- Human Resources - Personnel & Employment
- Health & Safety
- Insurance
- Management Documents
- Sales & Marketing Procedures

10. Finance

All franchisors should give prospective franchisees both profit & loss and cash flow forecasts for an absolute minimum of twelve months, ideally two years. They should be based on past performance but are only a guideline. You can use these figures or adjust them to suit your circumstances. They could be affected by such things as the amount of money that you have invested, loan repayments and working capital.

11. Exit Strategy

This might seem strange when you are just starting your franchise business, but every business person should have an exit strategy. There will be clauses in the franchise agreement covering things like death and national disasters, but what if it doesn't work? Nobody plans to fail but it is important to plan for the 'What if?' scenario, and have a back-up plan. Sometimes all that may be required is changes to your existing business that reduce your costs or boost your income. Other times, it may be that, despite your best efforts, you have to close the business.

On a positive note, if you are successful you still need an exit plan: Are you going to renew your franchise agreement after the initial term? When do you want to retire? Are you planning to build the business and then sell it? All these things need careful consideration. The next chapter will focus on writing an Exit Strategy.

 # EXERCISE:

Ask yourself the following questions:

Do I have a short term, medium term and long term plan for my business?

Do I understand the financial implications of running the business?

Do I understand the sales and marketing process?

Do I have an exit strategy?

 # ACTIVITY:

Write a Business Plan.

"AN IDEA IS JUST AN IDEA UNTIL YOU MAKE IT HAPPEN. IT'S NOT ABOUT IDEAS. IT'S ABOUT MAKING IDEAS HAPPEN."

Scott Belsky, co-founder of Behance

CHAPTER 11

WHAT IS YOUR EXIT STRATEGY?

When I ask prospective franchisees, "What is your exit strategy?" most of them are a bit bewildered. Some say, "I haven't even started yet," or, "I haven't got one," or, "I haven't even thought about it."

THE THREE D'S

To some, an exit strategy sounds negative. If your franchise business is your dream, why would you want to think about an exit? It's going to be so successful and so much fun that you don't need to think about what comes after. Wrong. There are several reasons why you need to plan an exit. Things change, and most changes can be summed up in what I refer to as the three D's. I have encountered each of them and can speak from experience.

Debt

Companies not paying on time or going bust, cash-flow problems, inability to pay off loans, banks withdrawing overdraft facilities and changes in the economy. All these factors can have a huge impact on a business and can ultimately lead to the business failing.

One of my own companies suffered a £69,000 bad debt in the fourth year of trading when our biggest customer was declared bankrupt by its Spanish owners. Up until that point we had doubled turnover each year, were profitable and had a very small overdraft facility, but that one act had a devastating effect on the business. Fortunately, we had a good relationship with the bank and were able to survive. We were back in profit after two years but the effect on the cash flow was huge.

One of the biggest problems for SME's in the UK today is cash flow; it can restrict growth and can also be caused because of growth. A company expanding rapidly will often need more investment, which often means more borrowing.

Disaster

Particularly recessions; the last recession had a massive impact on many businesses with hundreds of long-standing, established companies going out of business, and many more SME's ran by people of retirement age struggling to survive with no exit strategy. Recessions tend to happen every ten to twelve years as history repeats itself, and often business people are not prepared for it.

Losing a major customer can have a huge impact on a business. You have no doubt heard the saying, "Don't put all your eggs in one basket", but many companies have suffered or gone bankrupt for that reason. When a big company wants to do business with you it is hard to resist, but the consequences can be disastrous if they have a large percentage of your business. They will often squeeze you on prices, pay late and, when they want to change they will discard you. Take care when dealing with major brands.

Death or serious illness can obviously have an enormous effect on a business, especially if it is the owner, but also if it is a close relative of the owner. Often it is not expected and there is no contingency plan.

Divorce

There are hundreds of businessmen and women who have lost thousands and their business through acrimonious divorces. I am sure that you have read stories in the papers, usually about multimillionaires, but over 90% of businesses in the UK are SME's run by 'ordinary' people and divorce can have a devastating effect on both the business and personal life.

ON A MORE POSITIVE NOTE

Actually, the best reason for an exit strategy is to plan how to optimize a good situation, rather than get out of a bad one. This should be a fundamental part of your business plan. It allows you to run your business and focus your efforts on things that make it more appealing and compelling when the time comes to sell it.

Having an exit strategy is a very important part of anyone's business life and it can differ from one person to another. One might want to pass the business on to their children, while another might want to sell out and retire, and some just keep going.

You wouldn't dream of going into a railway station and asking for just a ticket to anywhere; the attendant would need to know where you are going! There is an old saying — "A man going nowhere, usually gets there… NOWHERE!"

As mentioned in the previous chapter on business planning, you should have a short-term plan, a five-year plan and a ten-year plan. After all, most franchise agreements are for five or ten years. These should then be broken down into shorter terms such as yearly and monthly.

Your exit strategy is usually linked to your goals, which can be both financial or personal, or a combination of both. The type of business you choose should depend on your goals, and the way you grow it should be aligned with your exit strategy. Don't wait until you are in trouble to think about an exit, rather think of it as a succession plan, or a successful transition.

 **EXERCISE:**

Ask yourself the following questions:

What is my exit strategy? What do I want to aim for when I leave the business?

 **ACTIVITY:**

Draft out an exit strategy. Look closely at it, considering all the possible outcomes and write down a clear plan of action, and be realistic.

"

"YOUR TIME IS LIMITED, SO DON'T WASTE IT LIVING SOMEONE ELSE'S LIFE.

DON'T BE TRAPPED BY DOGMA —
WHICH IS LIVING WITH THE RESULTS OF
OTHER PEOPLE'S THINKING.
DON'T LET THE NOISE OF OTHERS' OPINIONS DROWN
OUT YOUR OWN INNER VOICE.
AND MOST IMPORTANT, HAVE THE COURAGE TO FOLLOW
YOUR HEART AND INTUITION.
THEY SOMEHOW ALREADY KNOW WHAT YOU TRULY
WANT TO BECOME.

EVERYTHING ELSE IS SECONDARY."

Steve Jobs

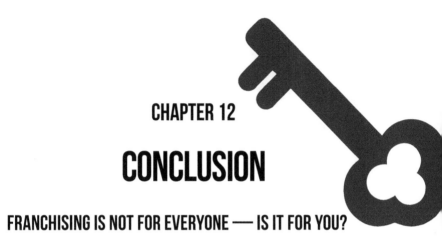

CHAPTER 12

CONCLUSION

FRANCHISING IS NOT FOR EVERYONE — IS IT FOR YOU?

Franchising can be a complex business for those who don't know the ins and outs. Buying a franchise can be a daunting task and needs careful consideration and becoming a franchisee is no guarantee of success, even with a major brand. It requires hard work, dedication, discipline, and a determination to succeed. Mistakes can prove costly but getting it right can rapidly take your business to a new level.

This book should give you all the tools and information you need to make an informed choice as to whether franchising is right for you and what type of franchise you should pursue. Also, by following my guidance, you stand the best chance of running a successful business.

If you are looking at buying a franchise, please take advice from a recognised franchise consultant, someone who has been there and done it. It will save you time and money... and possibly some heartache as well.

Plan and prepare, do your research, take your time, and find something that you will enjoy while you are making money.

Remember that franchising is a two-way street and both parties have obligations. Generally, you are investing in a proven system, so don't try to change it. If you are prepared to follow the system, then buying a franchise could be for you.

FINAL THOUGHTS

Before deciding to go down the franchise route, it is also advisable to take a step back and ask yourself once more the following six questions.

THESE SIX QUESTIONS CAN DEFINE YOUR FUTURE

1. What are you trying to achieve – What is your Ultimate Goal?
2. Why do you want to achieve this – What are your Motives?
3. When do you want to start and exit?
4. How are you going to achieve it?
5. Where do you want to be in 5/10 years?
6. Who is going to help you along the way?

I would love some feedback on my book and to hear some of your success stories as you embark on your new challenge. You can contact me on:

Website: www.thefranchisespecialist.co.uk

LinkedIn: Len Rainford

Facebook: The Franchise Specialist

Twitter: @LenRainford1

I sincerely hope that the information contained in this book has been helpful, but if you feel that you need to talk to someone on a personal level please give me a call for an informal chat. I am always happy to discuss any aspects of franchising.

All the very best in your search for the right franchise,

Len Rainford – The Franchise Specialist

"

"THE ONLY PLACE WHERE SUCCESS COMES BEFORE WORK IS IN THE DICTIONARY."

Vidal Sassoon

RECOMMENDED READING

How to Franchise Your Business by Brian Duckett and Paul Monaghan – The Franchising Centre

The easiest and least risky way to start your own business by Nick Riding – Franchise World.

The Franchising Handbook by Carl Reader

Guide to Franchising by Martin Mendelsohn

The Law and Regulation of Franchising in the EU by Mark Abell

Business Franchise Magazine

Elite Franchise Magazine

Franchise World Magazine

Making Money Magazine

What Franchise Magazines

Franchise recruitment websites

Franchise Direct . . . . www.franchisedirect.co.uk

Franchise Expo . . . . www.franchiseexpo.co.uk

Franchise Resales . . . . www.franchiseresales.co.uk

Franchise Sales . . . . www.franchisesales.co.uk

Franchise Supermarket. . . . www.franchisesupermarket.net/elite-franchise

Franchise UK . . . . www.franchise-uk.co.uk

Business for Sale . . . . . www.uk.businessesforsale.com/uk/franchises

Which Franchise . . . . www.whichfranchise.com

Websites of interest

The Approved Franchise Association . . . . www.theafa.org.uk

The British Franchise Association . . . . www.thebfa.org

The Franchise Specialist . . . . www.thefranchisespecialist.co.uk

ACKNOWLEDGEMENTS

There are so many people to say thank you to, and many will not even realise how much they have helped me over the years.

The franchise industry is quite a close-knit community and over the past 30 years I like to think that I have built some very good relationships and friendships with several business associates who have always been there with help and advice.

Joel Bissitt, Colin Chadwick, Pauline Cowie, Richard Davies, Brian Duckett, Iain Martin, Paul Monaghan, Kathryn Orange, Bill Pegram, Nick Riding, and Brian Rogan.

There are also many entrepreneurs and business people that have helped me along the way and have taken the time to share their expertise and business ideas.

Johnny Apples, Sian-Elin Flint-Freel, Steve Lythe, Andy Mault, Alistair McDonald, Ron Metheringham, Stuart Mitchell, Graham Philips, Alan Preston, Daniel Priestley, Alan & Rhian Spaven, Rowan Stone, and Linda Whitney.

Back in 2009 I decided to do the LEAD Management course at Lancaster University, where the Management School is ranked as one of the best in Europe. Several of my business friends asked me why I was doing it as I had already run four businesses. My answer was simple – you are never too old to learn. It was one of the best things that I have ever done, not only did I learn a lot, but I also met some very good business people who I am still friends with today. As a result of doing the programme I was asked to take part in some mentoring and do some lectures. I was then invited to become one of the first Entrepreneurs in Residence, which I consider a great honour, especially as I didn't even go to university when I left school. It gives me great pleasure to help the budding entrepreneurs of the next generation. To all the Entrepreneurs in Residence and all those that I have been involved with especially the following:

Dr Lola Doda, Dr Ian Gordon, Dr Magnus George, Dr Nigel Locket, and Dr Ricardo Zozimo.

When I first started in business we didn't have mentors or coaches as such like we do today but there are certain people that I have met and worked with over the years that I would class as real mentors for me personally.

Peter Wren, who founded and ran Outline Health Clubs back in the 1980's; Alan Jones, Managing Director of TNT in the 1980's; and Roger Baines, Managing Director of Amtrak in the 1990's.

THANK YOU

Lightning Source UK Ltd.
Milton Keynes UK
UKHW020628300819
348826UK00015B/975/P